Quick and Easy

REMO S TO
CUST OME

Disclaimer

To prevent accidents, keep safety in mind while you work. Use the safety guards installed on power equipment; they are for your protection. When working on power equipment, keep fingers away from saw blades, wear safety goggles to prevent injuries from flying wood chips and sawdust, wear headphones to protect your hearing, and consider installing a dust vacuum to reduce the amount of airborne dust in your woodshop. Don't wear loose clothing, such as neckties or shirt with loose sleeves, or jewelry, such as rings, necklaces or bracelets, when working on power equipment, and tie back long hair to prevent it from getting caught in your equipment.

The author and editors who compiled this book have tried to make all the contents as accurate as possible. Plans, illustrations, photographs and text have been carefully checked. All instructions, plans and projects should be carefully read, studied and understood before beginning construction. Due to the variability of local conditions, construction materials, skill levels, etc., neither the author nor Betterway Books assumes any responsibility for any accidents, injuries, damages or other losses incurred resulting from the material presented in this book.

METRIC CONVERSION CHART

TO CONVERT	TO	MULTIPLY BY
Inches	Centimeters	2.54
Centimeters	Inches	0.4
Feet	Centimeters	30.5
Centimeters	Feet	0.03
Yards	Meters	0.9
Meters	Yards	1.1
Sq. Inches	Sq. Centimeters	6.45
Sq. Centimeters	Sq. Inches	0.16
Sq. Feet	Sq. Meters	0.09
Sq. Meters	Sq. Feet	10.8
Sq. Yards	Sq. Meters	0.8
Sq. Meters	Sq. Yards	1.2
Pounds	Kilograms	0.45
Kilograms	Pounds	2.2
Ounces	Grams	28.4
Grams	Ounces	0.04

QUICK AND EASY

REMODELING PROJECTS

TO

CUSTOMIZE YOUR HOME

JACK KRAMER

BETTERWAY BOOKS

CINCINNATI, OHIO

Quick and Easy Remodeling Projects to Customize Your Home. Copyright © 1995
by Jack Kramer. Printed and bound in the United States of America. All rights
reserved. No part of this book may be reproduced in any form or by any electronic
or mechanical means including information storage and retrieval systems without
permission in writing from the publisher, except by a reviewer, who may quote
brief passages in a review. Published by Betterway Books, an imprint of F&W
Publications, Inc., 1507 Dana Avenue, Cincinnati, Ohio 45207. First edition.

99   98   97   96   95   5   4   3   2   1

Library of Congress Cataloging in Publication Data

Kramer, Jack
    Quick and easy remodeling projects to customize your home / by Jack Kramer.
        p.   cm.
    Includes index.
    ISBN 1-55870-336-5
    1. Dwellings—Remodeling—Amateurs' manuals. 2. Building—Details—
Amateurs' manuals. I. Title.
TH4816.K754   1995
643'.7—dc20   94-39853
                                                      CIP

Edited by R. Adam Blake
Designed by Sandy Conopeotis-Kent
Illustrations by Adrian Martinez

Author's Note

This book was started when my illustrator, Adrian Martinez, purchased a thirty-year-old tract house at a small cost. It was in almost impossible condition, but the basic construction was there. It needed window and door treatment, wall work and new floors. It needed ceiling work and a new entrance. In essence, it needed remodeling. The house was approached with an eye for aesthetics and an artist's touch. This book is mostly a chronicle of that house and how it became a home. Some remodeling details are from my own home and work.

My heartiest thanks to Adrian and Mary Martinez for allowing me to use their purchases as an example of how to make a home for little cost and some rewarding effort.

Introduction

Many houses on today's real estate market lack the charm and beauty that distinguish the dwellings of the past. Gone are the carved moldings, handsome windows and trim, and hardwood floors. Yesterday's skilled woodworkers and builders have been replaced by subcontractors installing mass-produced building components. The economics of modern construction do not allow for such amenities, but the desire for crafted beauty still exists. Adding features such as porches, patios, fencing and gates, and interior trim can *make* a home from a plain house.

The resurgence in the desire for personalized detailing has resulted in the proliferation of materials and products to satisfy that longing. Not everyone can build a house, but almost everyone can do something to add beauty, craft and personality to an otherwise drab or lifeless house. A sterile entranceway can become an inviting portal through the addition of an arbor or gate. The front door, usually bland, can become a hand-carved or stained-glass statement. And *there are* attractive replacements for the plain motel-style windows that plague so many fifties and sixties houses. Tired floors can be easily redone in parquet or hardwood. Decks and patios of very small proportions can dramatically alter the feel of a house; and don't forget the old-fashioned sun porch. Converted from a screened porch or added to a home, it creates a feeling of spaciousness beyond its small area.

The material cost for these finishing touches is not exorbitant, but the cost of hired labor is. If you do it yourself, however, you can afford quite a lot of home improvement. Forget the savings and consider the enjoyment of creating a new home with your own hands. Making your home an inviting, unique and handsome one is within your reach. With this book in hand, and with many drawings to help you along, you can transform your house into something surprisingly individual. Whether you have an old or new home that lacks that craftsperson's touch, this book is written for you.

CHAPTER ONE

WOOD

Wood can transform an ordinary house into an exceptional one. Casement windows, paneled doors and beamed ceilings all provide that enduring and desirable old-world charm we are always seeking. It is these finishing touches and other amenities you can build that make a house a home—a personalized place.

The wood we use in building is essentially from the trunks of trees, which contain sapwood and heartwood. Sapwood, the living part of the tree, is a very thin layer that entirely surrounds the trunk. Within the sapwood, the cambium layer carries water and minerals through the tree to the leaves. Heartwood is old sapwood that no longer contains growing cells that carry or store sap. The chemical changes that have taken place in the aging heartwood make it stronger and heavier than sapwood.

All wood contains natural defects: knots, splits and irregular grain. Because most of our work involves detailing and is readily seen, it is important that the wood selected be as perfect as possible—free of knots and splits—yet still have visual character. Select wood yourself, instead of ordering it by phone, so that you get exactly the quality you want. Before purchasing any wood, inspect it personally to be sure it is free of defects.

CHARACTERISTICS OF WOOD

Some woods are hard and difficult to work with, but others are soft and easily nailed into. Some woods cut more easily than others; some have a rich, natural coloring; and some others are light and uniformly grained. But all woods fall into two basic classifications: *hardwood* and *softwood*. These two terms refer to the growth and reproductive patterns of the trees and not to the hardness or softness of the woods they yield. Hardwoods come from deciduous trees (those that lose their leaves in winter), and softwoods come from conifers (trees that reproduce by growing cones filled with seed)—usually evergreens.

However, some softwoods such as southern pine and Douglas fir are actually harder than some hardwoods, such as poplar or mahogany. There's a difference between softwood and soft wood. The softwoods are generally less expensive and easier to work with than hardwoods; however—except for redwood and cedars—they are often less attractive. The softwoods are primarily used as structural components in houses, e.g., wall studs, joists and rafters, as well as in plywoods. The more handsomely grained hardwoods are more costly, but are preferred for most furniture, floor and interior work.

SPECIES OF WOOD

The names and classifications of wood create confusion because three important groups of people each have their own reasons for distinguishing between species. Botanists, lumber professionals and users of wood are not always speaking the same language. You can make better decisions about lumber purchases if you know a little about each group's way of naming wood.

Softwoods

PINE

Pine is a relatively soft wood, easy to nail and work with. It has a good resistance to shock and has dozens of uses both interior and exterior. It takes stain well; it is stable and remains intact under the pressures of drilling and screwing; and it is easy to shape. Many of the pines yield beautiful and dramatically grained lumber that was once used exhaustively for interior work such as finishing trim and flooring. It is now not as available as the firs, spruces and hemlocks, which are what most construction-grade lumber is currently sawn from. Often, no distinction is made between those species; and at the lumberyard or home-supply store, your lumber may be referred to by the generic catchall name *white wood*. Many people, even lumberyards, refer to these commercial woods as pine, but once you hold a 1 × 4 of white wood next to one of rich and satiny true red pine, you won't be satisfied with any old *pine* again.

DOUGLAS FIR

Douglas fir is plentiful, and it regularly grows to 200 feet, making it the most important lumber tree in America. But it is not a true fir. It is more closely related to the true pines and shares many of those characteristics, but it does not take finishing as well. It is a general building wood that is easy to work with and, because of the size of the trees, is available in high-quality lengths. This wood is excellent for joists, rafters, or anywhere a clean, long span is called for.

SPRUCE, HEMLOCK AND FIR

The separate species of spruce, hemlock and fir are often not distinguished in lumbering. Most of these trees are suitable for general construction work. Spruce is so soft that quite a bit of it goes directly into pulp production; hemlock, not as plentiful as spruce, is somewhat harder and tougher grained; and fir, which is usually lighter in weight, often finds its way to the plywood mills.

You will rarely encounter any of these woods being sold as varietal products in the construction lumber market; but when you go to buy general building lumber such as 2 × 4s or 1 × 6s or plywood, these are the families of wood that you will most likely be bringing home.

CEDAR

There are three basic "cedars" in use in the U.S.: western red, northern white and eastern red, none of which is really a cedar. Eastern red cedar is the one used in old hope chests and for lining closets. It is actually a low-growing juniper. The wood is very hard, but it is easy to work and extremely attractive with its natural deep-red coloring and wavy grain. Because it is not available in great dimensions, it is most often used as a furniture wood.

Western red cedar is the most commonly used outdoor wood. Northern white has become rarer as the eastern forests have been logged. The western variety is used for shingles, fencing boards and siding. It is easy to work, and it is very attractive in its natural colors and grain; however, it soon weathers to a silver gray out of doors. It will resist decay and insect attack, making it the most economical choice for garden and lawn uses. Beware, though: Cedar contains chemicals that will quickly decompose ordinary steel nails. Always use galvanized nails and screws on your cedar projects.

Cedar is also used for interior work. Because it is often sold with one rough side, it is commonly used for the rustic look.

REDWOOD

Redwood is the wood of choice for siding, fencing, and most outdoor uses where durability is called for. It is not a very hard wood, so it is rarely used where it might be subject to impact. It is a soft wood that does not take shock well, but it is easy to work with. It resists decay and termites and takes finishes well. Redwood is frequently used for outdoor projects because it is water resistant and is not a target of termites. Because of the limited sources of redwood, it has become increasingly expensive; however, it is well worth the expense for that special place in your home.

Hardwoods

ASH

Ash is used in baseball bats, and it was once used as the leaf springs in early automobiles, which should give you some idea of its strength. Ash has almost *perfect memory*, meaning that no matter how much or how long it is bent (but not broken) it will return to its previous shape. Like nearly all the hardwoods, ash is extremely hard and resists impact. It, like oak, is open grained; that is, the wood contains tiny openings along the grain. If you want a smooth, mirror-like finish, you must either use a wood filler on ash and oak or choose a smooth-grained wood.

CHERRY

Cherry heartwood is a deep red, but the outer sapwood that has not had time to age within the tree can be nearly blonde. If you have decided that you want that smooth, glassy finish, then cherry is your wood. It can be sanded down with 400-grit sandpaper to a lustrous glow.

MAPLE

Maple is the stuff that butcher blocks are made of. It's hard, dense and smooth grained. The drawback to working with maple is that it will quickly reduce your tools to a useless bluntness. Projects involving maple are best postponed until you have gained some experience and patience in woodworking.

POPLAR

Poplar is probably the softest of the hardwoods that you will encounter in regular lumber stores. It is easy to work, and it accepts and holds onto paint better than almost any other hardwood. Poplar also accepts finishes well, but the grain tends to look muddy and plain compared with other woods. This wood is not moisture resistant, so either keep it inside or keep it painted.

OAK

Oak is the most available wood you will find. The easiest distinction to make is between white oak and red oak. White oak is more attractive and has more grain characteristics, but red oak is usually much more plentiful and much cheaper as well. It is tough and hard, right on the heels of ash and maple, but it is a satisfying wood to work. It is an accomplishment to create a task in oak, and its natural, open-grained beauty makes it worth the effort.

WALNUT

Walnut is an excellent wood for indoor work. It works as easily as many softwoods, yet it is much harder and finishes beautifully. Most walnut is a dark, glowing brown, but, like cherry, some of the sapwood can be very light. It is slightly open grained, but it can be lightly filled to a smooth gloss.

Buy your walnut cautiously. It is the most expensive of the general domestic hardwoods, and you should carefully inspect any walnut that you buy. Beware of so-called good deals on walnut—especially when it is being sold by an individual. It may well be substandard lumber.

GUIDE TO MAJOR WOODS

Wood	Characteristics	Uses
Redwood	Known for resistance to weather. Good workability.	Exterior; posts, beams.
Cedar (several species)	Resists decay. Easy to work.	Exterior uses; interior paneling, trim.
Yellow pine	Very strong, stiff, good holding. Moderately easy to work.	Framing, trim, subflooring, interior paneling.
White pine	Light and soft wood. Very easy to work.	Interior finish, framing, cabinetry.
Douglas fir	Heavy, strong, good nail-holding ability. First choice for structural work.	Framing, sheathing, floors, posts, beams.
Ash, Oak	Hard, durable and extremely strong.	Furniture, trim, flooring. Use where strength is needed.
Maple	Very hard and dense. Difficult to work.	Countertops and wherever wood is likely to sustain impacts or abrasion.
Cherry, Walnut	Smooth textured and moderately easy hardwoods to work.	Furniture, trim, cabinetry, decorative items.
Poplar	Soft and easy to work. Holds paint well.	Exterior (with paint), windows, doors, cabinetry.

GRADING LUMBER

Lumber is graded on a varying scale: the top of the line is almost entirely free of visual flaws, and the bottom has some structural defects. Grading systems differ for various woods; for example, redwood is graded construction, construction common, Merchantable or Merchantable Heart depending on finishes and defects. Douglas fir is graded All Heart A, All Heart B, Grade 1, Grade 2—again the grading is dependent on appearance and soundness.

Even within the specific grades of lumber, there are so many variations that it is wise, as mentioned, to select your lumber yourself rather than having it selected for you. All of the various methods and schemes for lumber grading are too much to present here. Ask for a grading booklet at your lumberyard; many lumber producers publish them.

It is not uncommon for a few pieces of lumber to be warped, out of square, or to have some other defect that might make the board unsuitable for some uses. This is allowable in the building trade, where buyers are purchasing large amounts of wood to be used on larger projects, but it can wreak havoc for the amateur carpenter. The builder can always find the best way to utilize the imperfect pieces in such a way that the structure is sound and the wood is not wasted; but if you are using only a few boards, your options are limited. Remember that you are dealing with a product that is not at all homogenous. No amount of grading can make all boards the same. But that is part of the romance of working in wood. It is not mass-produced and uniform. Each piece of stock has its own character and demands that you pay attention to its peculiarities of grain and cut.

LUMBER DIMENSIONS

Since the actual size of a piece of lumber is not what the nominal dimensions say, here is a table of dimensions:

Size to order	Actual size
1 × 4	¾ × 3½
1 × 6	¾ × 5½
1 × 8	¾ × 7¼
2 × 4	1½ × 3½
2 × 6	1½ × 5½

PRESSURE-TREATED WOOD

Pressure-treated woods last longer than other woods. The process involves chromated copper arsenate or other similar chemicals forced into the cells of the wood by subjecting the wood to pressure or a vacuum. The process can be used on most woods, but Southern yellow pine, fir and hemlock are most commonly treated because of their receptivity to the process.

Be aware that pressure-treated wood contains toxic chemicals—after all, bugs, mildew and fungus can't survive in it. Use good judgment with treated wood where there will be long-term contact with the skin, and never use it as a food surface. The same goes for burning treated wood. Don't do it. In some localities it is considered a dangerous waste, and laws prescribe proper ways of disposing of the scrap.

PLYWOOD

Plywood is made from several layers of veneer (thin layers of wood) laid with each layer's grain perpendicular to the next and bonded together with synthetic glues. The thickness of the plies varies, depending upon what the wood is to be used for. Plywood is stronger than solid woods because of the crossing of the grains.

Some plywoods have core veneer of inferior quality; the joints between edges may not be perfectly mated; there may be knots or patches in them. The more expensive the plywood, the better the quality, and unless you are well versed in the grading codes of plywood (e.g., CDX, S1S, BCD), you should *always* select plywood in person. Plywood comes with both surfaces sanded or unsanded and is available in several grades, types and sizes; the smallest is 4′ × 4′.

Plywood Grading

INTERIOR KINDS
N — Smooth surfaced, all heartwood or sapwood; free of defects.
B — Solid surface; some minor splits and knots.
A — Smooth; can be used for natural finish. Most popular.
C — Tight knots, some splits.
D — Knots and knotholes to 2″ width across, limited splits.

EXTERIOR KINDS
A-A — Used for fences, outdoor structures; smooth finish.
A-B — One side not as smooth; good all-around outdoor use.
A-C — Also used frequently outdoors; one side may have knots.
B-B — Less expensive than others; some defects.

WHERE TO BUY LUMBER

Buying lumber can be confusing because it is available at lumberyards, at large home-improvement stores, and at the bigger hardware and home-supply centers.

The difference is most obviously price, but sometimes the cheapest place to buy is not the best place.

Lumberyards

If you feel lost in a conventional lumberyard, you are not alone; most home-owners scouting for a few boards seem to be in the minority compared to the professional carpenters (who do most of their ordering at lumberyards). However, invariably, the old-fashioned lumber house will give you personal attention, answer dozens of questions, and take care of your needs. Generally, you will be talking to experienced people. Take a sketch of the project you have in mind (you can use drawings from this book), and the salesperson will help you select exactly what you need. Lumberyards usually charge slightly higher prices than the home-supply centers, but often it is worth paying more to get the professional advice; furthermore, the lumber in stock offers a wide variety of choices. Lumber is the yard's bread-and-butter, so they stock consistent quality.

Home-Supply Stores

Home-supply stores, or home-improvement stores, are replacing the lumberyard as the most common source of building wood for the homeowner. What they offer is great convenience; that is, you can buy almost any type of hardware there along with your lumber, and the all-in-one-place shopping is a big plus. These outlets cater to the do-it-yourselfer, and even though the personnel may not be as experienced as the people at lumberyards, shopping at home-supply centers is very popular.

Usually, in these very large outlets, the lumber will be somewhat less expensive than at lumberyards (and not necessarily of lower quality). However, in the supermarket store, be aware that you are very much on your own. Although attendants may be on the premises, they can be difficult to find, and once found, may not be able to answer all questions you might have about your project. But they are selling hundreds of different products, so some allowance must be made for their sometimes incomplete answers.

The home-supply store or the lumberyard can usually deliver your purchase for a reasonable fee, but if you want to save money, provide your own means of transportation. If you do decide to take a delivery, it will be a tailgate delivery, meaning that the truck backs up and unloads the lumber on the spot and that you must cart it to where you are working.

CHAPTER TWO

WOODWORKING BASICS

Most people know how to use a hammer or screwdriver when working with wood. The techniques in this chapter will help you to use your tools more effectively and efficiently. (Note that some of the tools we mention are explained more fully in the next chapter.)

NAILS

There are many types of nails, yet it is important to use the right ones for the right jobs, or you will waste a great deal of time and material. You can purchase nails by bulk weight or in boxes or plastic packages.

The basic nail types are box, common, finishing and casing.

Common nails are used for general construction; the nail has a wide, thick head to take the stress of hard hammering.

Box nails are similar to the common nail but have a slimmer shank, which means that they are weaker but are less likely to split wood.

Finishing nails are used when you don't want the head of the nail to show. Their small head enables you to sink the rounded head with a nailset. The resulting puncture in the wood can then be easily filled or puttied over.

Casing nails are somewhat similar to finishing nails but have a thicker shank and more angular taper under the head. They are used for floor work.

For exterior use, rustproof nails such as galvanized are used. These nails are hot dipped into zinc, giving them a corrosion-resistant coating.

If you need rustproof nails, use galvanized, stainless steel, copper or aluminum nails. Try to always use a nail that measures at least 1⅔ as long as the thickness of the board you are using. Nails with sharp points are preferred over blunt-nosed ones, and thinner nails should be used for hardwood rather than for softwood.

Nailing

To brush up on your nailing techniques, use a scrap piece of lumber. With soft woods you can nail without making a pilot hole, but if you are using hard woods, you have to make a pilot hole with a drill. The pilot hole should be slightly smaller than the diameter of the nail and about two-thirds of its length. Hold the hammer near the end of its handle, and start the nail with light taps while holding it in place with your fingers. Once the nail is started, remove your fingers and take full swings, using the wrist and arm. If a nail bends slightly, change the striking angle to get the nail straight into the wood. However, if the nail bends severely, remove it and start with a new one. As the nail becomes level with the surface of the wood, ease up on the power.

To remove a nail, lift it out with the claw edge of the hammer (not as easy as you think). There is a small ledge at the bottom of the V between the claws; you must get this edge under the head of the nail. When the claw is engaged, roll the hammer on the curve of the head. Move the claw into a vertical position to lift the nail; let the claw loosen and move it at an angle; then insert a block of wood under the hammer head for leverage. Now apply pressure on the handle and remove the nail with a fast jerk. Some nails, such as finishing (casing) nails, have small heads that are difficult, but not impossible, to remove.

Nails driven at a slant hold better than nails driven straight down into wood. For an item with several parts, say, an intricate window, first clamp the wood pieces together and then nail. The clamp or vise lets you use both hands—one for holding the item, the other for nailing.

If you have to insert nails within one inch of the end of a board, drill a pilot hole first, or the wood will split. With some hardwoods or when using thicker nails, you must increase the distance from the end of the board that you can safely nail without first drilling a pilot. Driving nails closely together in a line can also split wood, so stagger the nail holes along different lines of grain. Always nail across rather than in between the grain. If joining two boards, be sure the nail is long enough to join them, but not so long that it goes through the boards. The length of the nail should be ¼″ less than the total depth of the two boards.

Whenever possible, drive nails on the inside of pieces of wood rather than on the outside so the nails will not show. Exposed nail heads are no disaster, but if they can be avoided, so much the better.

Toe nailing is driving a nail into wood at an angle, generally in corners or where nails cannot be driven from the outside. When toe nailing, start the nail about ¾ inches from the edge and drive it at a 45° angle. Practice this technique.

It takes some experience before you can accurately judge where a toe-nailed nail will end up.

SCREWS

There are many kinds of screws used for wood. The most common is the flathead, which sits flush with the wood surface. The flathead may be a slotted or a Phillips screw; the cross pattern in the Phillips screw head keeps the screwdriver from slipping.

Roundhead screws have a flat bottom under the screw head so that they sit atop the wood surface. The oval head screw is like a combination flathead/roundhead. You can buy screws from ¼" to more than 3" in length, and they are available in different finishes, including the corrosion-resistant screws used for outdoor work. Screws can be installed using a standard drill driver, a screw gun or an electric screwdriver. The modern battery-operated drill/screw gun has made the hand turning of screws unthinkable to most woodworkers. If you don't have one now, think seriously about purchasing one. They are available in a broad price range; and once you own one, you'll instinctively use it rather than reaching for a plain old screwdriver.

Installing Screws

Always use screws the proper length and width for the thickness of the wood—you do not want the end of the screw protruding from the wood. It is difficult to install a screw without a predrilled pilot hole. The pilot hole should be slightly smaller than the diameter of the screw used. For the screw to hold in the wood, the entire length of the threaded part of the screw should penetrate the base piece.

Flathead and oval-headed screws must be countersunk so that the widest part of the head is flush with the wood surface. To do this, drill a beveled hole equal to the diameter of the screw head. If you do not own a countersink bit, find a drill bit that is as close as possible to the exact size of the screw head—but not any larger. Drill this hole after you do the pilot hole for the screw; thus, you have to drill two holes for countersunk screws (unless, of course, you have bought a combination countersink/pilot bit). If you wish to conceal the screw head, then you must drill the countersink deeper so that a plug can be inserted into the surface of your piece. This takes some preplanning and careful matching of screw, countersink and plug.

Driving a screw into wood is a simple operation if you have matched the screwdriver to the shape, width and length of the slot(s) of the screw. Otherwise it can be a mess. If you are using an old, muscle-powered tool, use the screwdriver with a firm grip and a steady turning motion that is directly in line with the path of the screw, neither too hard nor too soft. If the screw seems too hard to drive into the wood, use a little bar soap or candle wax on the threads to lubricate them. Try to keep screwdrivers sharp and properly shaped. (You can file heads to make them smooth.)

GLUES

Today there are excellent wood epoxies and glues that make joining boards and attaching wood members quite easy. Some are miraculously strong and could *probably* be used by themselves without any other fasteners, but it is wise to drive a few nails in place.

Select a heavy-duty glue recommended by hardware store personnel. If you are going to do extensive gluing, it will be necessary to hold the pieces of wood together while the glue sets. You can use clamps, which are sold at hardware stores, or hold the pieces in a vise until they set.

When you apply the glue, try to put it exactly where the joints come together; do not get it all over the wood. Be on target, and use just enough so that when the pieces of wood are pressed together, only a slight residue escapes at the edges. Immediately wipe off excess glue with a cloth. When using glue from a plastic squeeze bottle, be sure to evenly spread the lines of glue over the surfaces being joined. Use any kind of spreading tool that will do the job: plastic, cardboard, a wood chip, or even your fingers if you have a wet rag to wipe them off with.

SAWING

To start a saw cut, hold your thumb right at the mark you've made. Brace the side of the saw against the side of your thumb, and draw the saw back, making several short cuts. The simple, first cut will make sawing easy because the saw then has a guideline cut to get it moving. Now, holding the saw at a 45° angle to the top surface of the wood, saw with long, easy strokes, neither too fast nor too slow. If you feel that the only way to get the saw to cut is to press and push down on the handle, then your saw is dull.

Nothing can end a budding woodworking career faster than unsuitably dull tools. The teeth of your saw should feel knife sharp when you slide a thumb

HOW TO MEASURE AND SAW WOOD

Measuring and sawing wood well requires more than just a board and a saw. You need a solid surface for the piece, practice, and, most of all, a *sharp* saw.

The correct way to mark with a square is by holding a pencil tilted slightly.

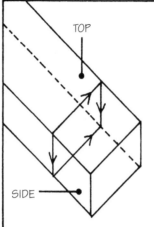

For the perfect square cut, run top, bottom and side lines in the same direction.

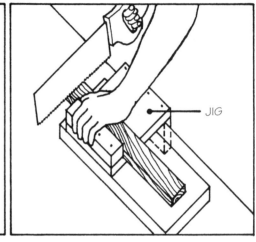

A bench hook jig helps to steady small wood.

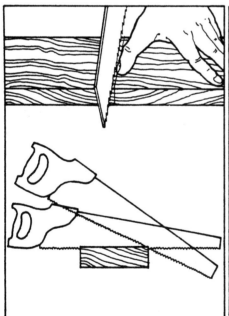

To start the cut, steady the saw with your thumbnail and draw back several times until the blade "locks" into the cutting pattern. Cut at a 45° angle.

During the cut, steady the lumber with one hand. Before the cut is completed, hold the cut-off piece to avoid splintering.

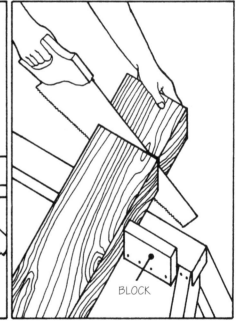

Cutting heavy lumber requires the safety of a block support or a C-clamp against hazardous movement.

and forefinger down its length. If the points of the teeth appear to have shiny, rounded ends, then get your saw to a sharpener before you ruin both your wood and your enthusiasm for the project.

Once the saw is moving, keep up the stroking and cutting, letting the saw and easy pressure do the work. If the saw leaves the line, turn the handle slightly so the blade can get back to the guideline. To guide a saw for an accurate cut, use a block of wood with a squared end held flush to the side of the blade.

I've been discussing the way to handle a crosscut saw—that is, going across the grain. But when using a ripcut saw—a saw that has widely set teeth and is meant for sawing along the length of the grain—hold the saw at a 60° angle to the wood: place the handle higher in the air. No matter which way you are cutting, when you get close to the end of the wood, support the cut-off piece to prevent splintering of the last unsawn portions.

Use the coping saw for curved cuts; hold the wood in a vise vertically and point the teeth of the saw so that they aim *away* from you. Thus, the cut is made with the push stroke.

If you are cutting a thin slice from the end of a board, place the board on a piece of scrap. Start the cut in the scrap board and follow through. If possible, clamp the two boards together to prevent tear-out.

MAKING WOOD JOINTS

Probably the most important aspect of wood construction is joinery, and there are a variety of ways to do it. The most common and easiest joint for the beginner is the *butt joint*, which is put together straight, with a scab nailed across the joint, or right-angled, one end capping the other, and is nailed or screwed in place, one piece of lumber to the other. Sometimes glue is used in addition to the nails or screws. The butt joint eliminates the angled or mitered cut, but for aesthetics—where you want a neat appearance—the mitered cut is best. In the *miter cut*, no end grain is visible. The miter is cut with a miter box, at a 45° angle. The miter joint is not as strong as the butt joint, so it is most often used where appearance, not strength, is important. Whichever you use, plan ahead for sound joinery and for uniform visual effect.

The *lap joint*, frequently used, is easy to do. The lap joint is an *L* shape; you cut away a section of one board and a section of the joining board and then put them together like a sandwich. This joint is usually glued and nailed. There are several variations of the lap joint, such as cross-lap and middle-lap joints, but the principle is the same: a recess is cut in one side to hide most of the grain, and the board is set flush in place and glued and nailed.

JOINTS

Basic wood joints each have special purposes that take advantage of the strength of the grain. No joint will do in every situation. Looking at the grain and thinking about the direction of stress on the joint will tell you which method is best.

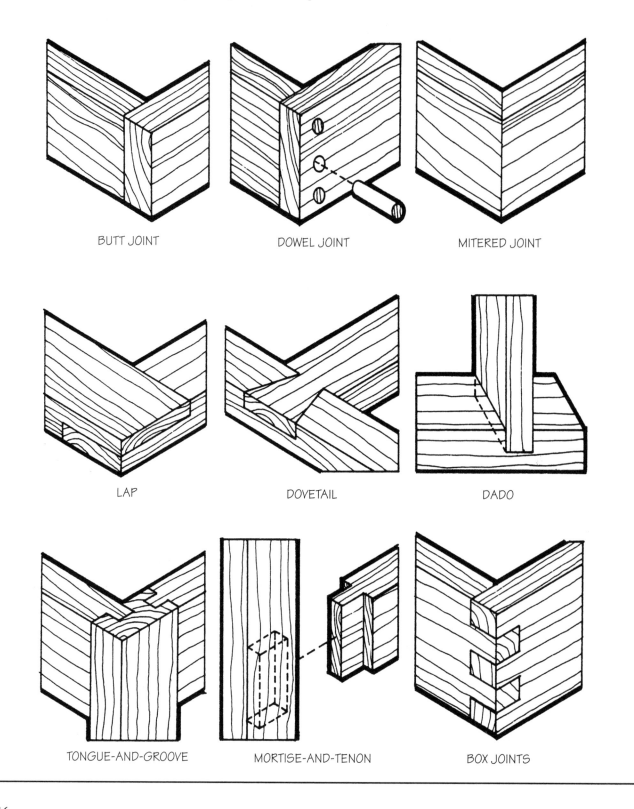

BUTT JOINT   DOWEL JOINT   MITERED JOINT

LAP   DOVETAIL   DADO

TONGUE-AND-GROOVE   MORTISE-AND-TENON   BOX JOINTS

A *mortise-and-tenon joint* is exceptionally strong; this is a *T* shape. The mortise is the slot on the left piece of wood, and the tenon is the tongue on the right. This is fitted into the mortise with glue.

There are many other types of joints, but basically these are the ones you will work with.

WOOD TERMS

Perhaps better called *construction terms*, these are various words used to describe the pieces in standard construction. For each part of house construction — doors and windows, floors, ceilings, walls — there are terms for describing the wood members; a working knowledge of these terms will help you in ordering lumber and in doing construction. When we talk of walls, we talk about *studs* and *top plates* and *sole* (or *base*) *plates*. Window and door construction includes words like *trimmer stud*, *header*, *sill* and *jamb*. Ceiling work uses *beams*, *rafters* and *joists*; and in floor work, there are *joists* and *subflooring*. Illustrations on the next pages show some of these parts and their names. At the beginning of later chapters, you will find a glossary of terms that are used in or that apply to that chapter.

CONSTRUCTION PARTS

The names of construction parts are special to the building trades, and most carpenters expect you to use them properly. Using the right term marks the insider from the outsider.

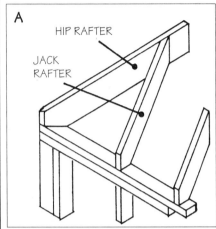

A

HIP RAFTER

JACK RAFTER

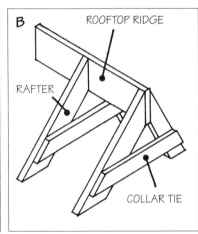

B

ROOFTOP RIDGE

RAFTER

COLLAR TIE

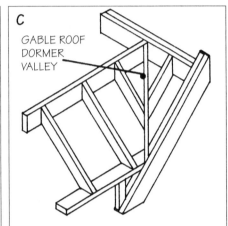

C

GABLE ROOF DORMER VALLEY

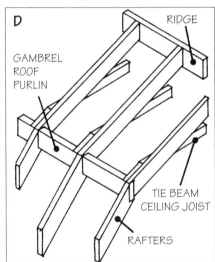

D

RIDGE

GAMBREL ROOF PURLIN

TIE BEAM CEILING JOIST

RAFTERS

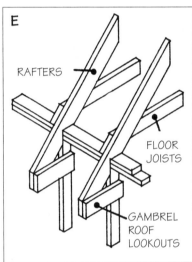

E

RAFTERS

FLOOR JOISTS

GAMBREL ROOF LOOKOUTS

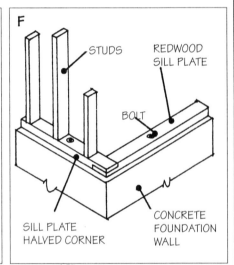

F

STUDS

REDWOOD SILL PLATE

BOLT

SILL PLATE HALVED CORNER

CONCRETE FOUNDATION WALL

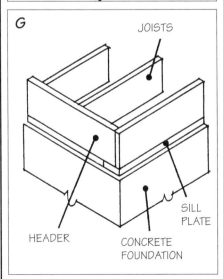

G

JOISTS

HEADER

CONCRETE FOUNDATION

SILL PLATE

A Hip and jack rafters
B Rooftop ridge and collar tie
C Roof valley on gable roof
D Purlin on gambrel roof secured by tie-beam joist
E Lookouts on gambrel roof
F Sill plate halved corner
G Header and joist on sill plate

CONSTRUCTION PARTS

The names of construction parts are special to the building trades, and most carpenters expect you to use them properly. Using the right term marks the insider from the outsider.

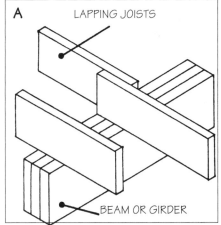

A — LAPPING JOISTS — BEAM OR GIRDER

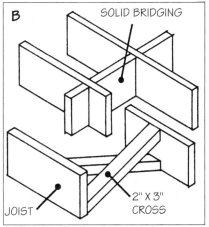

B — SOLID BRIDGING — JOIST — 2" X 3" CROSS

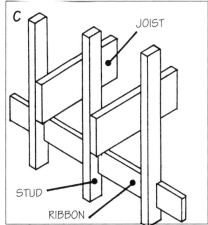

C — JOIST — STUD — RIBBON

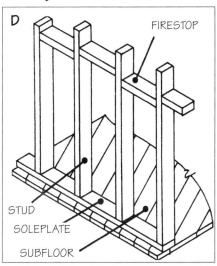

D — FIRESTOP — STUD — SOLEPLATE — SUBFLOOR

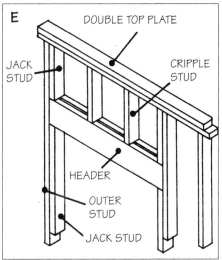

E — DOUBLE TOP PLATE — JACK STUD — CRIPPLE STUD — HEADER — OUTER STUD — JACK STUD

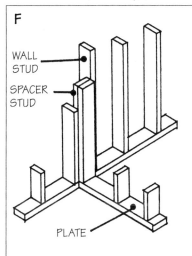

F — WALL STUD — SPACER STUD — PLATE

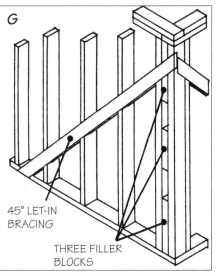

G — 45° LET-IN BRACING — THREE FILLER BLOCKS

A   Floor Joists on wood beam or girder

B   Floor joists secured by bridging

C   Ribbon-bearing joists

D   Firestop (fireblocking) between studs

E   Window or door header with cripple and jack studs

F   Spacer stud for partition wall

G   Diagonal let-in (notched into studs and corner) braces and three filler blocks in corner-post construction

CHAPTER THREE

GETTING STARTED

BUILDING CODES AND PERMITS

This book is concerned with making various structural changes — arches, skylights or windows — to an *existing* home, rather than building complete houses or rooms. However, the added features and finishing touches discussed here must be done according to local building codes. You may need various permits from your local building authorities. If you are doing most of the work yourself, you will need to know what building/construction restrictions are in effect in your area. Though most communities conform to national standard codes, all localities differ in defining work that requires permits or inspections.

BUILDING CODES

Certain building codes apply to almost all aspects of home remodeling or construction. The codes are created as engineering studies that define the design, strength and use of materials. Various construction manifestos may be referred to in your local regulations, and it all may seem overly complicated, but these codes are designed to ensure that your remodeling or building jobs result in safe and sanitary conditions. Building guidelines are laws that must be adhered to in any construction project. These regulations are set by planning boards, commissions, and other city officers who decide upon standards that are specific to the climate and geography of the jurisdiction.

Before you decide to install a new archway in your home, add a few skylights, or replace a wall or windows, check with your local building and planning office (generally located in city hall or county offices). Get phone numbers from the phone book or from your professional tradesperson if you are using one. Even better, visit the office in person. Ask for general guidelines or any other printed materials that your building department publishes. Write down the names of people you deal with in case you have more questions later or want to call the office in the future. As in any business, personal relationships are the best tools for resolving issues.

Grandfathered and Historical Codes

If you are altering an old house constructed before certain building codes were adapted, some exceptions may be in effect. Still, I strongly suggest that you check with local boards because building codes may vary from state to state, and even from town to town within a state. The "grandfathering" of certain conditions is not an absolute guarantee against legal orders to update, alter or cease certain uses of a structure. It is a simple matter for a building department to dispense with the grandfathering of things like outhouses, dirt floors or open crawl spaces.

If your house is in an area affected by historical codes, you may be surprised to find out that things like aluminum screen doors, horizontal boarded fences, and your favorite shade of blue have been outlawed. Historical codes may not be related to sound construction methods or to safe and sanitary building designs, but they are laws nonetheless.

PERMITS

You may need permits to do the work in this book. You should take your ideas, plans and working drawings to the local government building to find out. In some states, if you do the work yourself and the materials do not cost more than $500, no permits are necessary. Before you can secure a permit, you will need a sketch of what you are doing. This sketch does not have to be a detailed architectural drawing—just a general sketch—but officials usually require that you show your lot lines and the perimeter of your existing house along with the drawing of proposed work. Minor alterations or repairs usually do not require permits. However, if you are removing a wall or altering the roof by adding skylights, for example, do check with the building office to be sure you do not need a permit. Otherwise, if a neighbor reports you or if officials discover you are making or have made alterations without the proper permit(s), you may be fined, issued a "stop work" order, or, worst of all, ordered to tear out the work you've already done.

FINANCING

Many of the projects in this book—putting in posts, installing new flooring or adding a sun-room—fall within the scope of a home remodeling loan. These equity loans are currently easy to secure if your credit is good; and the interest on them can usually be deducted from your personal income tax. Check with your accountant for up-to-date information. Note, however, that these loans are second mortgages, so borrow only according to your means. You don't want to lose your house should you lose your job.

Do It Yourself

Generally, all the projects discussed here can be built by anyone handy with tools, or by you and a carpenter working together. You do not need a general contractor for the projects described here. You can replace a window yourself, install a tile floor, lay parquet flooring, or add an arbor or trellis to the garden, and do it successfully. All of these activities are within the realm of do-it-yourself work.

If you want, with this book and its working drawings in hand, you can approach a carpenter for an estimate on your job and let the carpenter do all the work if you are not handy yourself. Even if you are handy, you may not want to spend the time doing the work, so hiring a carpenter is a good alternative. Working along with a carpenter is another option. Knowing more about construction methods and terms, and understanding what goes into a project, will help you strike a better deal for yourself and for the contractor. Most tradespersons would rather deal with a customer who understands the work than one who has little understanding and even less trust.

SAFETY FACTS

1. Be sure you have a safe electrical setup.
2. Read labels on paint containers and other chemical products.
3. Wear eye protection when sawing, nailing, demolishing or painting.
4. Never lift more than you can *comfortably* handle.
5. Keep your hands away from ends of cutters, blades and bits.
6. Hold a portable saw with *both* hands.
7. Do not work with small pieces of stock if you can avoid it.
8. Always work in sufficient light.
9. Work with well-sharpened tools; keep them clean.

10. Never use a power tool without clamping or securing the workpiece.
11. Never use a part of your body to support a workpiece when you are cutting with power equipment.
12. Be careful when carrying pointed or sharp tools.
13. *Always* check your local building codes; codes protect you and public safety.

CHAPTER FOUR

WOOD TOOLS

SAWS

The saw is the universal cutting tool; you can use reliable (well-sharpened) handsaws or the more convenient and faster power saws. A lot of tools today are both inexpensive and available to novices. The handsaws used in small carpentry work are the crosscut saw, the ripsaw, the backsaw, the compass saw and the coping saw. Some examples of power saws are the circular saw, the saber saw, the reciprocating saw, the band saw, and the power miter saw. A coarse tooth is better on thicker and softer woods; a fine tooth gives a cleaner edge. Also, a narrow blade cuts tighter curves than a wide blade.

Handsaws

The standard crosscut saw is the handsaw you will use most. Used for cutting across the grain, it is narrower at the tip than at the handle. The ripsaw has more teeth per inch (TPI), and the teeth are set wider apart than with the crosscut saw.

The compass, or keyhole, saw has a V-shaped blade about 12 to 16 inches long secured in a small, rectangular frame. It is used for accurate cuts and curves. Another type of compass saw, the coping saw, makes fine-curve cutting easy. The end of the blade is held by a loop or pin. A backsaw looks like a handsaw but has the same width blade at the handle end and a thick, rigid lip along the length of the top of the saw. It is used for cutting joints and for general bench work.

PORTABLE POWER TOOLS

A power saw may cut with a circular blade, a continuous band, or a short stiff blade, as in a reciprocating or saber saw. The circular saw is for straight cuts;

continuous band and reciprocating saws are for cutting curves. In usual parlance, the larger-capacity saws having free blades are differentiated from saber saws. Generally, the saber saw accepts a blade up to 3 inches in length, and the reciprocating saw will use blades up to 15 inches long. The larger saws are often used only in the demolition phase of work. A saber saw is highly recommended because it is basically a portable scroll saw. Because the end of the blade is free, it can cut both enclosed and external curves. The saber saw blade is stiff but not long, and it works on an up-and-down motion. The band saw, used for cutting both irregular and straight shapes, comes with a choice of blades. (Various types of power saws are also available as table models.)

Circular Saw

The circular saw is the most universal carpenter's power tool. It is compact, powerful and versatile in the hands of someone with experience. In the hands of an overconfident novice, however, it is dangerous. With respect and patience, you can learn to use this tool on most of your projects.

The circular saw most often accepts a 7¼″ blade, which is fine for 2 × 4s, but it will not cut all the way through a 4 × 4 in one pass. It is excellent for crosscutting, ripping, panel sawing, and for trimming fixed boards. Just as with a handsaw, the most important thing is to keep a sharpened blade. If you hit a nail or hard mineral surface, the blade is probably shot. Buy plain steel blades at first; then, when your skill level increases, you can begin to add special-purpose, carbide-toothed blades to your collection.

Power Miter Saw

In recent years, the power miter saw has become a standard tool for most carpenters. It is basically a hand-held circular saw on a spring-loaded mount with a fence and table beneath it. Wood is placed under the upright saw. The woodworker squeezes both the handle and trigger at once, and the saw blade is pushed down into the stationary workpiece. When the trigger is released and the saw is allowed to spring back into its up position, the blade brakes itself quickly, allowing the work to be removed. Power miters are portable and make extremely well-controlled and accurate cuts.

Reciprocating Saw

The reciprocating saw is a great power tool for cutting-in windows and skylights, and it operates like a freehand saber saw. Various blades enable you to cut wall

POWER TOOLS

The availability and improvements in power hand tools is what has made home improvements possible for the novice . Still, practice and care are necessary.

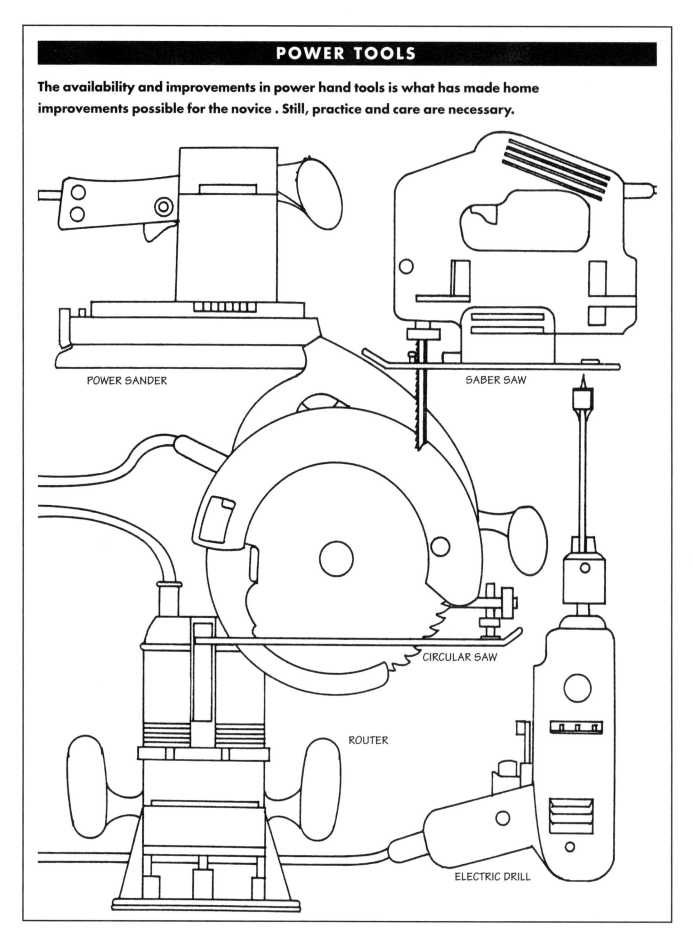

POWER SANDER

SABER SAW

CIRCULAR SAW

ROUTER

ELECTRIC DRILL

studs, plaster, even steel. The saw has two speeds and sometimes a variable-speed trigger. Blades vary in length and tooth size. Usually 4 to 10 tpi works best on wood. When operating this saw, keep a firm grip on the handle with one hand. To eliminate vibration, keep the blade guard pushed hard against the matcrial you are cutting. The reciprocating saw is an expensive tool, so if you need one, you might consider renting.

Power Drills

The electric drill is as essential to remodeling as are the hammer and screwdriver. You can use an old-fashioned hand drill, if you can still find one, but the power drill is easier to use and far superior. If you have a small hand drill (these are the egg-beater-type drills that use up to ¼″-diameter bits), by all means don't throw it away — it might be an antique.

The most common electric drill has a ⅜″-diameter shank capacity; the diameter refers to the size of the neck that clamps around the bit. You want a drill with a geared-key-type chuck to center and grip the bit. Check local hardware stores for drill attachments, especially bits for driving screws and for all-in-one pilot and countersink bits.

DRILLING

When drilling, use an easy pressure, letting the bit do the work. Try not to overheat the drill by using excessive pressure and speed. Just like your saws, your bits must be kept sharp. Remember that when you think you need to push hard against the material in order to get the job done, your bits or blades need to be replaced.

To drill a hole, mark the diameter of the hole and its exact position on the wood with a pencil; keep in mind the depth you want to drill into the wood: halfway through, one-quarter through, completely through, and so forth. For the most accurate drilling, use a nail or a nailset to make a starter hole. Place the drill firmly in the center, and pay careful attention to holding it perpendicular to the wood before you pull the trigger. Work on a waist-high, level table. Drill easily but steadily until the desired depth is reached. If you need to stop drilling at a particular depth, wrap tape around the bit at the desired distance. If you are drilling large (over ⅜ inch) holes, you should invest in an inexpensive set of *spade* bits. Or if you have the money, auger bits do the best job in wood boring.

Follow the safety rules that come with a drill, keep your shirt tucked in, and always wear goggles when drilling to protect your eyes from flying debris.

Battery-Powered Drills

Battery-powered drills are a great convenience and enable you to work without hindrance of wires. Few tradespersons would go onto the jobsite without one these days. Some power drills have removable batteries; others come with charger stands. They are made under a large variety of trade names, so be sure to inspect all models before buying.

STATIONARY POWER TOOLS

Table Saws

The basic table or bench saw is the table saw, which is used for straight-line cutting, crosscutting, and ripping long boards. By tilting the blade, you can achieve bevel cuts of any angle up to 45°. The saw has a sturdy table, an arbor (a protective hood), and a motor; the blade is secured to the arbor and driven by a motor with belts and pulleys. There are numerous circular saw blades, from crosscut to ripsaw.

Radial Arm Saw

The radial arm saw does basically everything the circular saw does and has the extra advantage of being easy to use because it cuts from above the work. Layout marks are always in view on top of the wood. The tool remains stationary while the saw blade is moved over the work. This tool has a yoke-mounted motor suspended from a horizontal arm; the arm is mounted on a sturdy column at the rear. The motor, yoke and horizontal arm can be adjusted to any desired angle. With various accessories, the radial arm saw can grind, sand, shape and rout.

Band Saw

The band saw makes bevel cuts up to 45°. With this saw you can easily do compound cutting and pattern sawing. The blade is of flexible steel, and the ends are welded together to form a continuous band. The blade is set over two large wheels that automatically track the path of the blade. If you enjoy pattern cutting and intricate work, a good band saw might be a worthwhile investment. They are vertical machines, so they don't need a lot of space. They usually run on ordinary house current, and they are not as noisy as most other power saws.

Scroll Saw

The scroll saw is actually a motor-driven coping saw and, like the band and saber saws, makes irregular cuts. Its advantage is that it can do fine precision work. The machine has a very fine, thin blade held between two chucks, one below and one above the worktable. It, like the band saw, is an excellent saw for hobbyists. It is small, relatively quiet, and lends itself to intricate work.

Electric Sanders

Portable electric sanders are of the belt type and the finishing type. Belt sanders work quickly on rough wood, especially good for large areas. The finishing sanders go at high speeds to produce a very fine finish. When using the belt sander, always keep the sander moving when it is on the wood. Move the sander back and forth with the grain of the wood. Lift off at the end of each pass and start again. Belt sanders are available by the width and length of the belt— 4″ × 24″ is probably the most useful for most *rough* jobs. Beware of belt sanders on your fine projects: they can destroy hours of work and hundreds of dollars of materials in less than a minute. Never use a belt sander on a finished surface until you have practiced on scrap or nonsurface material.

HAND TOOLS

Hammers

There are dozens of hammers available, from upholsterers' hammers to the standard household hammer. Claw hammers are available in two types: the curved and the ripping. The curved claw is preferred because it provides more leverage when you are pulling nails. The ripping claw hammer has claws that extend in more of a straight line from the head, and like the name suggests, it's good for ripping—drywall, old boards or general demolition work.

A patternmaker's hammer is also an invaluable tool to have on hand for making small items. A 6-ounce one is just about right. A small upholsterer's hammer is helpful because it has a narrow head, weighs little, and can get into places that the standard claw hammer cannot reach. Hammers come in long and short lengths. The long ones give you more leverage, and the short ones are ideal for more ordinary work. Hammer weights also vary. A 14- to 16-ounce hammerhead is fine for most finish work and suits most people. If you are doing framing or using 16-penny nails, you might want to find a 21-ounce hammer, but in any case, use a hammer that feels good in your hand.

Screwdrivers

Even though battery-operated screwdrivers have nearly taken over all screwing jobs, you need to have some hand-helds. There are dozens of sizes and kinds of screwdrivers available. Buy four or five with different-sized heads: an ill-fitting screwdriver can lead to trouble as well as frustration. The blade of the screwdriver should fit snugly into the screw slot. If the screwdriver fits too loosely, it is almost impossible to drive the screw in properly. Buy the large, standard-type screwdriver with a square shank, and remember that a long screwdriver gives you more power than a short-handled one and is less likely to tilt in the screw slot. Buy the best screwdrivers that you can; those made of soft or inferior metal are less than worthless.

Marking Tools

Good tools for marking cuts on wood are a good, heavy lead pencil and a ruler—you will use both these tools repeatedly. Always use a sharp pencil to mark lines, being careful to angle it toward the work.

The *combination square* can be used as a level, marking gage or depth gage. The handle slides along a channel in the blade. With a small knob, you adjust the distance the handle moves.

A *chalk line* is a long, spool-wound cord fitted into a container filled with chalk. The string is pulled from the container, stretched across a piece of wood, and snapped downward, leaving a straight, chalk-mark line.

A *marking gage* marks lines parallel to a board. The gage has a thick, rounded rule that can be tightened down at any specific mark. A mark is scratched with a sharp pin at the edge of the rule as the block rides along the board edge.

A very important tool is a *wing divider*. This tool lays out round lines, such as rounded corners. It is also useful for making circles and arcs. A wing divider looks like the old school compass; the difference is that there are two metal-edged points, and the distance between the points is adjusted by a screw device.

Planes

You will need a plane to remove unwanted portions of wood from a board or molding. As opposed to a chisel, you can control the depth and width of the cut with a plane. The bench plane and the block plane are used for general carpentry.

The block plane is small, can be manipulated with one hand, and is used for smoothing with the grain along a board's length. Bench planes come in three sizes: the jointer plane, the jack plane and the smooth plane. A long plane is best because it smoothes wood easily; short ones have a tendency to ride up and

HAMMERS AND SCREWDRIVERS

Hand tools are still the mainstay of woodwork. No power tool can replace the hammer, the chisel or the hand plane.

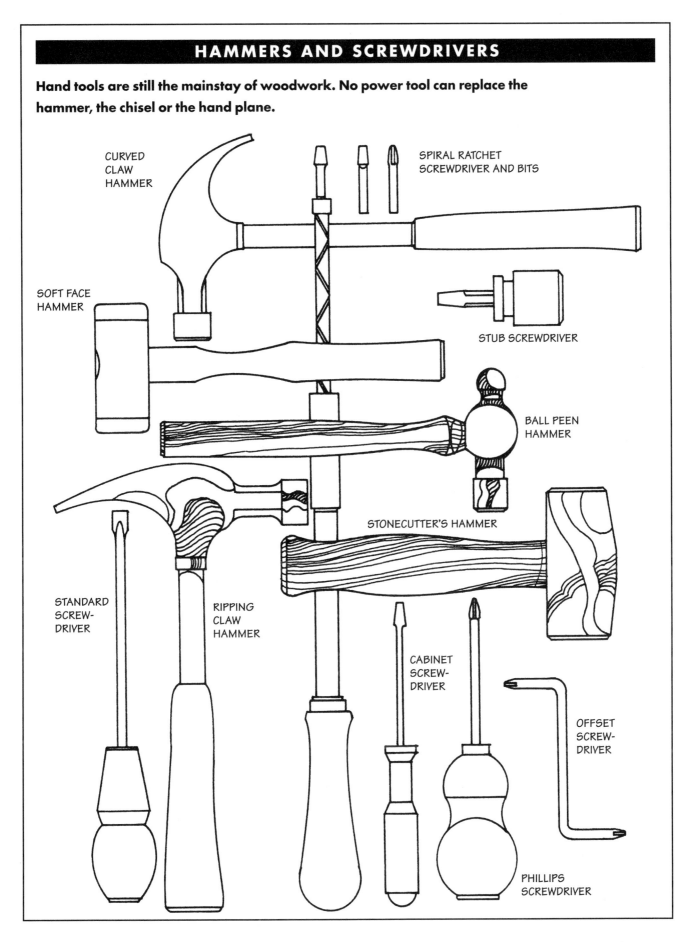

CURVED CLAW HAMMER

SPIRAL RATCHET SCREWDRIVER AND BITS

SOFT FACE HAMMER

STUB SCREWDRIVER

BALL PEEN HAMMER

STONECUTTER'S HAMMER

STANDARD SCREW-DRIVER

RIPPING CLAW HAMMER

CABINET SCREW-DRIVER

OFFSET SCREW-DRIVER

PHILLIPS SCREWDRIVER

HAND TOOLS

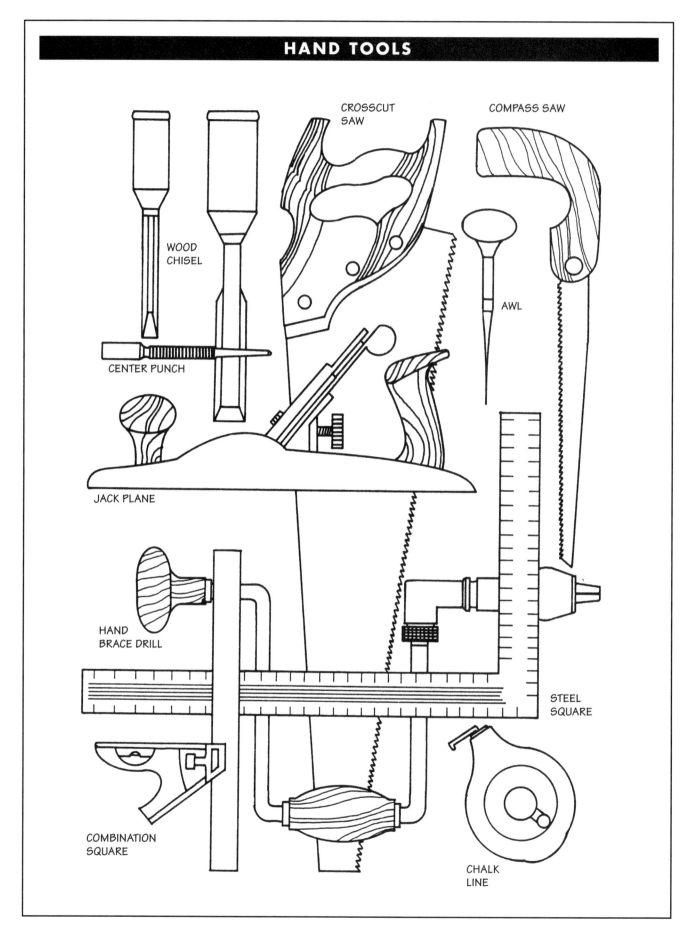

CROSSCUT
SAW

COMPASS SAW

WOOD
CHISEL

AWL

CENTER PUNCH

JACK PLANE

HAND
BRACE DRILL

STEEL
SQUARE

COMBINATION
SQUARE

CHALK
LINE

down. The jack plane is the best for our work and measures from 12 to 15 inches; it is excellent for removing irregularities on wood. The small bench plane is about 6 inches long and is used for smoothing surfaces after the jack plane has been used. Electric hand planes, also available, are convenient to use.

It is important to know exactly how to use a plane or you will ruin the wood with it. Sight down the plane's underside, and be sure the blade edge is protruding only slightly through the opening and is perfectly square across. If it is not, adjust it with the screw cap until it is. Angle the bench plane to get a shearing cut, and always cut in the same direction as the grain of the wood. Keep the cuts shallow but always even. Use more pressure at the front knob, and plane in short, even strokes.

Once again, sharpness is everything. Most people who think that they cannot plane wood have never tried it with a properly sharpened tool. The *iron* (as a plane's "blade" is called) actually shaves the wood, so it must be razor sharp in order to do its job. If you don't know how to sharpen the iron properly, take it to a professional sharpener. Maybe you'll want to learn how to do it yourself — if not, investing in an extra iron as a spare is a good idea. I never plane unless my iron is sharp enough to literally shave the hairs on my forearm.

Clamps

You need various clamping tools to hold pieces of wood together when you drill, nail or glue them. Whenever you use clamping tools, protect the wood surfaces you are working on by fitting lumber between the jaws and the wood block.

The woodworker's vise is perhaps the most useful of the holding tools; this versatile tool clamps onto a workbench or table and holds many materials securely so you can work on them. Buy a vise with large jaws, and when bench- or table-mounting a vise, keep the top of the jaws flush with the tabletop.

The C-clamp, another useful holding device, has jaws from 3 to 16 inches apart. The C-clamp can be attached to a workbench or to several pieces of work. There is a wide selection of clamps, and they are necessary for steadying glued pieces until set. To protect wood surfaces from injury by jaws of clamps, put a piece of wood or leather between the jaws and the surface you are working.

C-clamps hold work to a bench or sawhorse, and spring clamps are fine for fixing scrap guides and for light work. A third type, bar clamps, have a sliding jaw for clamping across wide surfaces. There are other holding and clamping tools, but usually the vise and C-clamps are all you need for woodwork.

Other Equipment

In addition to the standard tools, you will need a pair of sawhorses, which you can build from 2 × 4s or buy. Here is a case where I suggest you buy instead of doing it yourself. It is essential to have a good sturdy sawhorse to hold wood while you cut. I still use my old homemade ones, but the folding metal sawhorses are more durable and easier to carry around.

You will need ladders—generally one 12-foot ladder and an extension 16- to 24-foot type. Remember that the measurement of an extension ladder refers to its total (and not all usable) length. A 32-foot ladder will extend to about 25 feet, but that's probably all you'll ever want to climb. And besides, the gutters on a two-story house are usually only 18 to 20 feet from the ground. If you need scaffolding, of course you will need two ladders the same size; but you can rent both scaffolding and ladders.

Tarpaulin cloths come in handy for covering and protecting finished areas of construction. *Tarps*, as they are called, are expensive, so you might want to use the inexpensive plastic sheeting sold at paint stores—or raid the family rag bag for old bedspreads or sheets. If you are putting in a skylight, you won't want to mar the finished floor; the tarp protects it. Use it.

A wheelbarrow comes in handy for dozens of jobs when you are remodeling. You, of course, transport things in it, but it can also be used for mixing mortar. By all means get the best wheelbarrow you can afford; the cheap ones invariably fall apart in a few short months.

RENT-IT SHOPS

Today there are rent-it shops in most neighborhoods; here you can rent tools and equipment you do not want to buy—say a reciprocating saw or another costly tool. Rental is often by the hour or the half day. Generally a deposit is necessary, and when you return the tool, your deposit is refunded. Rental shops are convenient and great for the occasional do-it-yourselfer who does not want to spend too much money on a certain project and only infrequently engages in remodeling.

HELPFUL HINTS

Tools are one thing, but a good friend to help you when you are remodeling is another. If possible, have someone give you a hand. Many construction jobs, such as handling a 4' × 8' piece of plywood, really require four hands. Handling long rafters and beams if you are redoing a ceiling also requires the help of another person. And if you are working on a ceiling, you will realize that two people can do the job in less than half the time. It saves one person's running down and up the ladder to get lumber. Sometimes all you need is someone to hold one end of a board while you nail it.

One last thing: Although we do not anticipate accidents when you work with wood and tools, you are likely to sustain cuts and bruises. Keep a good first-aid kit on hand. (Nobody is perfect.)

CHAPTER FIVE

ARBORS AND ARCHWAYS

Too often, when people start to rebuild or remodel a home, they forget a very important aspect of good, total planning. Busy with the interior of the house, they neglect the approach to the house, yet this is where the guest first gets an impression of what is to come. The entrance, walkway or approach to the house can and does reflect what is inside the home; it is vitally important to the overall plan. The beauty of arbors, loggias or pergolas (besides their obvious attractiveness) is that they provide an old-world charm to an entrance. What's more, adding small details like an arbor or an archway can be done in a weekend.

CONSTRUCTION LANGUAGE

ARBOR: An open-ended, light structure often covered with vines, branches or climbing shrubbery.

BENDERBOARD: Thin, flexible veneer.

CLEAT: Metal hardware, usually U-shaped, applied to wood to support another piece of wood.

GIRDER: A heavy beam of wood used as horizontal support and supported by columns.

LEDGER: A strip of lumber.

LOGGIA: A roofed, open gallery in the side of a building.

NAILING BLOCK: A strip of wood attached to a surface to provide means of attaching another member by nailing.

PERGOLA: An open-roofed structure, usually with parallel colonnades and cross rafters.

PIER: A column of masonry.

TOENAILING: Nailing at an angle.

TRELLIS: A structure made of latticework.

ARBORS

The arbor, the craftsman's tour de force in old England, was the introduction to many a charming cottage. These structures have dimension and beauty, and they provide a restful, shady area—a place to pause before going inside. With an arbor, you do not need a gate, and the arbor serves as an additional small living area, as it defines the property. It is also a guidepost that says, "Welcome."

Because it is so visually prominent, the arbor must be built with the utmost attention to detail, pattern and proportion. True, you can crisscross sticks in any pattern and still come out with a reasonably charming effect, but the carefully executed arbor is a stunning sight. With arbors, you are working with specific designs, so preplanning on paper is definitely necessary.

What distance from the house should the arbor be placed? There is no hard-and-fast rule. Experiment by having someone stand at different points and see which works the best.

The basic construction of arbors requires trellis work, sticks nailed into a diamond or grid pattern. You can buy ready-made arbors—commercial units made mainly of wire and metal. Commercial garden suppliers carry them, and you'll find many styles and types. Generally, these units are expensive, and you still must put them together.

TRELLISES

As long ago as the eighteenth century, Italian and French gardens used trellises as effective decoration. The use of the crisscross wood designs has continued through the years, and today trellises are considered natural additions to a garden. With foliage or flowering plants, a trellis can define a boundary or become a screen or "tapestry" of color that enhances any garden area and adds great charm to the total home-and-garden picture.

A standard trellis consists of lightweight wood strips, or *lath*. Lath should be redwood or cedar, about ⅜" thick and 1" to 2" wide, in lengths of 6', 8' or 10'. Lath is purchased in bundles containing anywhere from 10 to 100 pieces. Surfaced lath is best because it is relatively free of splinters, knots or blemishes. You can construct a trellis from *battens*, which are thicker than ordinary laths: ½" to ¾" and 1" or 2" wide. Battens are available in lengths of 20', in bundles of 20 or 30 pieces. Battens cost more than redwood or cedar laths but are sturdier. The tradeoff is that battens may not be cut from redwood or cedar and will be subject to decay sooner.

Trellis Construction

Trellises are not difficult to make; they are constructed by nailing and gluing (with waterproof glue) crisscross pieces of wood or by stapling the pieces using a heavy-duty staple gun. The diamond design is the most popular for a trellis; the rectangular or box design is also attractive. Most important in building a trellis is achieving uniform spacing so plants have sufficient space to grasp wood

ENTRANCE ARBOR

A well-built entrance arch can dramatically change the mood of your home. Be sure to select posts that are large enough. If 4 x 4 posts seem too small, by all means go to 6 x 6 or even 8 x 8 posts. They will lend substance and solidity to your house.

1 Cast concrete footings in place with metal post connectors.

2 Temporarily brace 4 x 4 posts in position and bolt to connectors.

3 Set 4 x 4 girder on posts, toenail and add 4 x 4, 45° braces. Attach 2 x 4 ledger to house wall.

4 Taper one end of 2 x 6 beams, space 24" apart and toenail in place.

5 Nail 2 x 2 cross pieces 16" apart, on top.

Note: Use redwood and galvanized nails.

18"　　　8' - 0"

4 X 4 GIRDER　　2 X 2s

2 X 2 LEDGER

4 X 4 DIAGONAL BRACE

HOUSE WALL

6' - 8"

4 X 4 POST

BRICK PAVING

CONCRETE FOOTING

SECTION

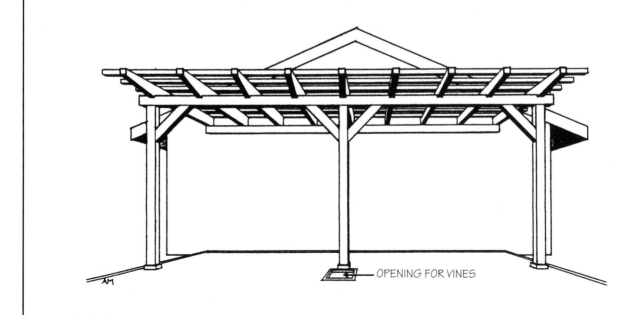

OPENING FOR VINES

and thus grow in a definite pattern. The spacing is calculated as follows: for ½"-thick lath, spacing should be ¾". For 1"-thick lath, spacing should be ¾". For 1½" × 1½" stock, a 2" space works well. Use a block of wood and insert that same wooden block in between each lath or batten to achieve uniform spacing as you nail laths in place.

Determining the amount of lath needed for your project can be a mind-twisting exercise if you try to approach the problem theoretically. The best method is to simply draw your pattern on paper and calculate from there. If your trellis is to be 6' tall and use 1" lath with ½" spacing, simple math (or a simple drawing) tells you that you'll use eight pieces of lath for every foot of width. So, eight pieces times 6' in height gives you 48' of lath for every foot of trellis length. Do the same for your cross pattern, and then buy about 20 percent more than you calculate to account for breakage or error, or to use to build a small trellis for your tomatoes.

You need framing to support the trellis. Use 2 × 4s for the top and bottom plates. Side plates can be 1 × 3s or 2 × 4s or 2 × 2s. Once you have constructed the lattice frame (somewhat like a framed picture), the frame must be anchored to the posts. Use 4 × 4s for posts, making them at least 24 inches longer than the actual vertical frame, to allow at least 16 to 24 inches to be set into concrete in the ground. The posts holding the trellis are set into the ground the same way fence posts are installed. Nail or screw all wooden members together. With a screw gun and galvanized screws, you should have a sturdy and durable trellis.

If you buy ready-made trellises, purchase those made of cedar. Commercially made trellises are available in two thicknesses; buy the thicker because it will long outlive the other. Pine can also be used, but it is not as strong or as durable as cedar and will need to be painted often.

Patterns

The grid pattern is the easiest to make. Using your spacer blocks, simply nail, screw and glue the vertical lathing to the top and bottom members; then repeat the procedure, nailing the other horizontal laths to each of the side pieces.

The basket-weave pattern is handsome but somewhat difficult to build. The laths are flexible, but alternate your assembly procedure from vertical to horizontal pieces, or you may find it impossible to weave over the full length of the trellis without breaking laths.

The diamond pattern is a variation of the grid and somewhat more difficult to make. Decide upon the angle you wish to create, and then cut a piece of plywood to act as a master marking tool.

Geometrical and star burst effects are also possible, but these patterns require *precise* laying out of the structure on the ground, nailing together and attaching

ARCHED TRELLIS

Trellises are basically latticework structures. The arched trellis makes a romantic statement, but trellises can be simple, free-standing uprights for roses and other climbers.

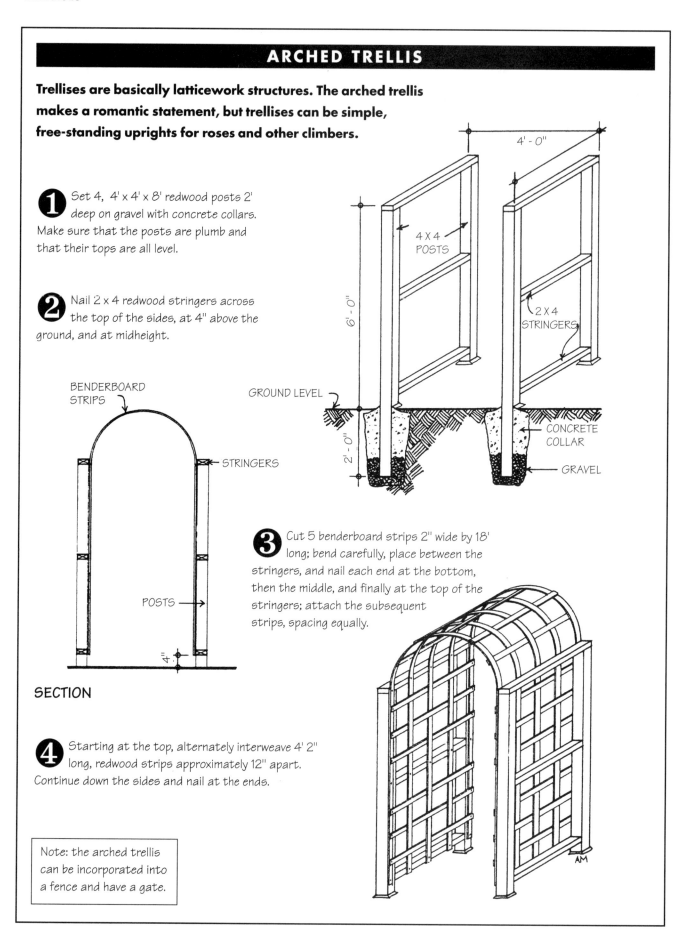

❶ Set 4, 4' x 4' x 8' redwood posts 2' deep on gravel with concrete collars. Make sure that the posts are plumb and that their tops are all level.

❷ Nail 2 x 4 redwood stringers across the top of the sides, at 4" above the ground, and at midheight.

BENDERBOARD STRIPS

STRINGERS

POSTS

SECTION

4' - 0"

4 X 4 POSTS

2 X 4 STRINGERS

6' - 0"

GROUND LEVEL

2' - 0"

CONCRETE COLLAR

GRAVEL

❸ Cut 5 benderboard strips 2" wide by 18' long; bend carefully, place between the stringers, and nail each end at the bottom, then the middle, and finally at the top of the stringers; attach the subsequent strips, spacing equally.

❹ Starting at the top, alternately interweave 4' 2" long, redwood strips approximately 12" apart. Continue down the sides and nail at the ends.

Note: the arched trellis can be incorporated into a fence and have a gate.

to frames. Because they are exterior, decorative items, trellises escape the constraints of the building inspectors. So if you have the inclination to create dazzling Victorian effects, here is your opportunity. When you are driving through an older neighborhood, pull over and walk; the best illustrations of trellis work are to be seen in person.

ARCHWAYS AND PERGOLAS

The *trellis archway* brings the beauty of the curve into focus at the entrance to the house. The archway is a tunnel placed strategically so it is focused on the doorway of the home. It adds perspective, relieves the bareness of many entrance grounds, and provides a unique effect, which is why it is now being used more than ever to give character to homes built in the fifties, sixties and seventies.

Archways require somewhat more construction than arbors, but the construction usually consists simply of straight sides on a series of posts. The overhead can repeat the curve pattern or have the flat-roof effect of trellises. To make the arch top, use benderboard—this is a redwood-veneer material that can be bent to shape by means of progressive nailing or screwing along its curved, supporting members.

A *pergola* is a structure that frames a view or adds interest to a house entrance. A pergola is similar to an archway but has heavier members and is less complicated in pattern. The pergola must be built with a strong framework because it makes a heavier statement than an arbor; thus, proportions must be preplanned thoroughly (i.e., drawn on paper). The pergola must have enough headroom for a person to walk under, as well as space for plants on top that are trailing downward; it must be wide enough for two people to walk abreast. The length of the pergola can vary, but it should never be confined; a 4-foot pergola simply will not look right. A pergola needs a length of at least 6 feet, although 10 feet is better so it can perform its function as an entranceway.

Pergola and archway posts should be 4 × 4s at a minimum, placed 6 or 8 feet on center to support the main framework; 3 × 4s can be used for the transverse beams above, but for visual effect, consider what type of plantings you intend to use. Always anchor posts to concrete piers that are set into a concrete footing.

See Drawings 5-3A and 5-3B for a step-by-step working plan of a pergola. This plan incorporates a deck and gives the house a handsome appearance. The roofing used on the pergola is optional; it may be open or it may be designed to serve as protection from sun and rain.

BUILDING AN ENTRY DECK AND PERGOLA

This entry and pergola will fit in almost any house. Large and spacious entry structures are not always possible. Remember that if you extend the girder length, you will need to increase the girder size.

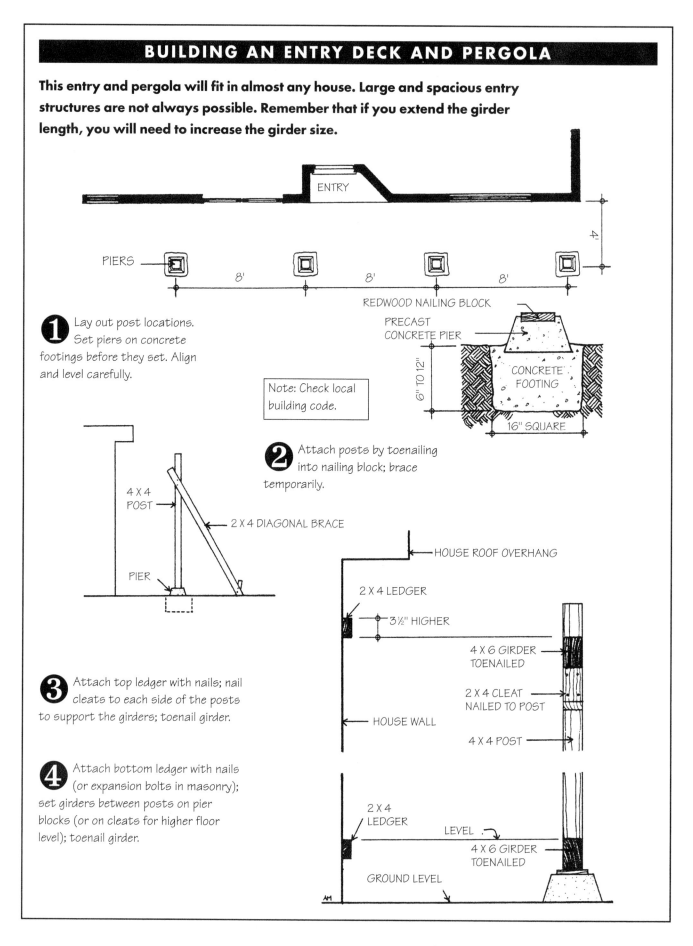

PIERS

ENTRY

4'

8'   8'   8'

REDWOOD NAILING BLOCK

PRECAST CONCRETE PIER

CONCRETE FOOTING

6" TO 12"

16" SQUARE

1 Lay out post locations. Set piers on concrete footings before they set. Align and level carefully.

Note: Check local building code.

4 X 4 POST

2 X 4 DIAGONAL BRACE

PIER

2 Attach posts by toenailing into nailing block; brace temporarily.

HOUSE ROOF OVERHANG

2 X 4 LEDGER

3½" HIGHER

4 X 6 GIRDER TOENAILED

2 X 4 CLEAT NAILED TO POST

HOUSE WALL

4 X 4 POST

3 Attach top ledger with nails; nail cleats to each side of the posts to support the girders; toenail girder.

4 Attach bottom ledger with nails (or expansion bolts in masonry); set girders between posts on pier blocks (or on cleats for higher floor level); toenail girder.

2 X 4 LEDGER

LEVEL

4 X 6 GIRDER TOENAILED

GROUND LEVEL

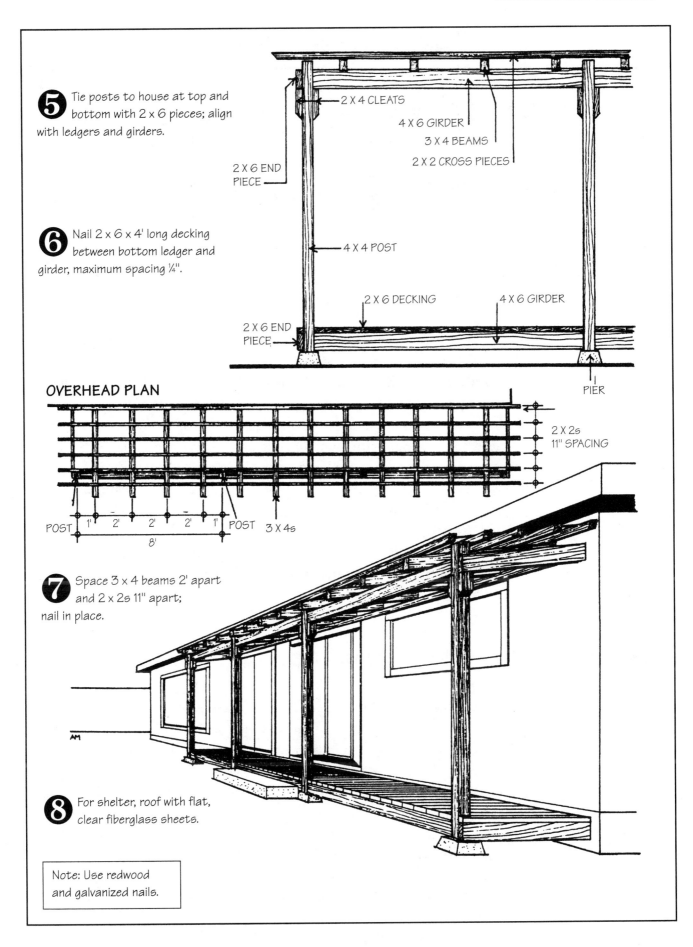

5 Tie posts to house at top and bottom with 2 x 6 pieces; align with ledgers and girders.

2 X 4 CLEATS

4 X 6 GIRDER

3 X 4 BEAMS

2 X 2 CROSS PIECES

2 X 6 END PIECE

6 Nail 2 x 6 x 4' long decking between bottom ledger and girder, maximum spacing ¼".

4 X 4 POST

2 X 6 DECKING

4 X 6 GIRDER

2 X 6 END PIECE

PIER

OVERHEAD PLAN

2 X 2s 11" SPACING

POST 1' 2' 2' 2' 1' POST   3 X 4s

8'

7 Space 3 x 4 beams 2' apart and 2 x 2s 11" apart; nail in place.

8 For shelter, roof with flat, clear fiberglass sheets.

Note: Use redwood and galvanized nails.

CHAPTER SIX

DOORS AND WINDOWS

Historically, doors and windows have been of many styles. Unfortunately, today's designs are so severe and simple that doors and windows have practically no character or craftsmanship. Yet these two necessary elements of a home provide the easiest way of restoring some beauty and style. Doors are not just exits and entrances, and windows are not just means of lighting. With some ornamentation and remodeling, they can come alive and contribute to the home's overall charm. For example, doors and windows can have flat lintels if the distance to be spanned is small; they can have arched heads if the distance is greater. Greek openings are defined by the lintel, Roman by the lintel and the arch, Gothic by the pointed arch, and Renaissance by the lintel and round arch. Adapting some of these classical lines to today's openings will give your house the distinct and appealing character that you may be seeking.

DOOR AND WINDOW OPENINGS

The classical Greek and Roman openings are rectangular and consist of jambs and a flat head framed with flat or molded caps or cornices. The faces of the jambs and the lintels provide surfaces that can be decorated to accent the opening. These small touches—the moldings—can create an extravagant door. By breaking the molding at the top, that is, by extending it beyond the door on each side at the top, you can achieve dimension and stability. The classical openings can assume many decorative accents. It depends on your skill and just how fancy you want to get.

Arched openings, hardly seen in today's architecture, are quite handsome. The tops of the arches can be heavily detailed and framed, and you can decorate

CONSTRUCTION LANGUAGE

BEAM: A horizontal timber used for support.

BEVEL: An angle cut on piece of wood or glass.

BLOCKING: A small piece of 2 × 4 lumber.

CRIPPLE STUDS: Vertical 2 × 4s above and below window openings.

FLASHING: Sheet metal set where a roof meets a wall; acts as weatherproofing.

FOOTING: A concrete platform installed below the frost line.

FOUNDATION: A wall, usually masonry.

FULL-HEIGHT STUDS: Vertical 2 × 4s running from floor to ceiling.

HEADER: A beam or board set at right angle to floor joists to form the top of an opening for a door or window.

JAMB: The sides and top of a frame around a window or door.

JOIST: A length of wood that supports a floor or ceiling. Joists are set on edge and are arranged at regular, parallel intervals.

LINTEL: A horizontal member spanning and usually carrying a load above or below an opening.

MORTISE: A slot cut into wood to receive another piece of wood.

MUDSILL: A base plate used at the bottom of windows and doors; usually 2 × 6, laid flat.

MULLION: A vertical divider between windowpanes.

RAFTER: A beam that supports a roof.

SHEATHING: A type of exterior surface of wall.

SHIMS: Tapered pieces of wood.

SHINGLES: Red or white cedar sawn to a taper.

SOLEPLATE: The bottom horizontal board, usually 2 × 6, at floor line.

STUD: A vertical member, usually 2 × 4, used in framing.

SUBFLOOR: A rough, wooden floor; the finished floor is laid on top of this floor.

TIE ROD: A rod used as a connecting member.

TOP PLATE: A horizontal board doubled, usually 2 × 6, above door and window openings, and supporting second-floor joists or roof rafters.

TRIMMER STUDS: Vertical members on sides of window and door openings.

them in many ways. It is embellishment upon embellishment, which today, of course, would look foolish, but *some* of the details can be used to create unique entrances.

The Gothic openings are somewhat more refined and narrower in structure than the Greek and Roman ones, but they are still quite ornate. They are perpendicular and more in scale with things than the large, Romanesque arched doorways and windows.

The Renaissance opening perhaps has had the most influence on today's architecture; its basic elements are adapted from the Greek and Roman styles. Gothic openings have the Roman pilasters, columns and arches, but they are refined by triangular-shaped lintels and rounded arches above the doors or windows.

This is only a glimpse at past treatments of doors and windows; we no longer use them today, but some degree of these effects certainly deserves a place in your home. We have stripped windows and doors of any detailing until they now look sterile; it is time to pay some attention to the eyes and ears of a building and to create more individual effects for our homes — for the sake of ourselves and our visitors.

DOORS

Doors are, of course, a means of entering a house or room, but remember that most of the time they are seen closed. Too many people forget that a door creates an impression. Think for a moment about doors you have seen: You remember those, perhaps, that had stained-glass highlights, those that were hand carved, and others that also had some distinguishing character. So what you want for your home is a handsome door, not just the flat, stock doors sold at mills.

Wood Doors

There is an incredible variety of wood doors, and each type of door has a certain character. Interior doors are available with one panel or as many as fifteen; arrangement of the panels varies. The more panels, the more ornate the door. Just what type you should use depends on the other house appointments. A three-paneled door is always handsome, and the six-paneled, colonial-type door has a warm feeling. The fifteen-paneled door is more elaborate but attractive in bigger homes.

Entrance (exterior doors) may be paneled, have glass sections, or be a combination of paneling and glass. The paneled exterior door, which is substantial, tends to give a formal look to a house. A paneled door with a bas-relief effect can take on many variations. What you select is dictated by what you can find. Try to find old doors at wrecking companies and salvage stores. Old doors are thicker and wider, and they last years longer than today's standard milled door because they were made better.

If you cannot find old doors, you can buy the *old-looking* doors manufacturers sell. (I should warn you that these doors are expensive.) Shop carefully, and always buy a door that is at least 2 inches thick; a heavier door not only looks better, but it feels better when you open it. And do not get carried away by an overly elaborate door. A simple pattern may look more elegant than a complicated one.

Glass Doors

The beautiful glass doors of yesteryear are again appearing in homes. These doors have beveled glass panes set in mullions; four stained-glass panes combined with clear-glass panes; or etched glass panes. A solid wood door with glass sidelights is another variation. Any glass door has a European flavor and is usually oversized. The eight-, ten- or twelve-paned glass French door with wood mullions is quite popular; it provides just enough glass but not too much. French doors are rich looking and beautiful. (We discuss how to hang French doors in the installation section farther on in the chapter.)

Look for old doors at salvage places. If the glass is broken, think about buying the door anyway, because you can always have the glass replaced with a pattern of your own choice (glazing a door is not hard). Beveled-glass panels are difficult, but not impossible, to find; several glass companies now stock them, or your local glazier can order them for you. Stained-glass doors are sold at antique shops, or you might want to make your own.

If you live in an area where burglary is a problem, forget glass doors. You'll be heartbroken if a thief knocks out a pane so he can try to reach inside for a spring lock.

French Doors

Frame up an opening for French doors (in pairs) by placing a 4×6 header and cripple studs as shown in Drawing 6-1. Put in 2×4 trimmers and the studs and soleplate. Allow for the door frame (usually 3½ inches), and also allow ¹⁄₁₆ inch around the doors at the sides, top and between. Leave ½ inch at the bottom. Shim doors in place; mark doors and jambs for hinges, and mortise them, using hinge halves as templates. Hang doors by aligning hinge leaves to each other and inserting pins. Mortise flush bolts into the ends of the door, and install the knob and lock into the other end. If necessary, plane the doors with a hand plane so they are smooth and even. Use weather stripping on all sides and the threshold.

Recessed Doors

A recessed door is a clever way of creating dimension and providing an interesting entrance to a home. The door is set back, providing a small corridor effect, which makes the entrance intimate. A door positioned in this manner eliminates the need for a visitor to walk directly into a room. There is a sense of entrance; and although the remodeled entranceway still has the door opening on the room, the outside entry provides an illusion of entrance. The entryway can also provide an L-shaped corner in the room, also creating charm. (See Drawing 6-2.)

Installation

Putting a new door in place or hanging it was once a complicated job, but not today. If proper stud framing exists, hanging the door should take only a small amount of time. The prehung door frame is like a box with a door hinged to it. This lets you slip the box into a stud-framed opening and secure it easily. Each prehung frame has two side jambs and a head jamb at the top. The doorstop or the molding runs around the inside of the jambs, and a sill and threshold are needed at the base of the two side jambs. The sill slopes away from the door base to keep water out.

REPLACING A DOOR

Replacing a door takes patience — even for professionals. Make sure that you have your sawhorses handy so that you can work on the door without needing to balance it at the same time.

1 Remove the existing door, leaving the hinges on the jamb (or replace them).

2 Measure the opening — the door should clear ⅟₁₆" at the sides and top and ½" at the bottom. If the replacement door is:

   A. Too big: cut down or plane the edges.

   B. Too small: glue equal wood strips to the ends.

WOOD STRIP   DOOR   WOOD STRIP

3 Shim the door in place, and using the hinge leaves as templates, mark and mortise the door, then secure the hinge leaves.

4 Bevel the latch side slightly toward the inside.

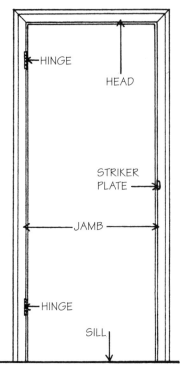

HINGE

HEAD

STRIKER PLATE

JAMB

HINGE

SILL

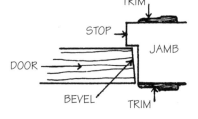

TRIM

STOP

JAMB

DOOR

BEVEL

TRIM

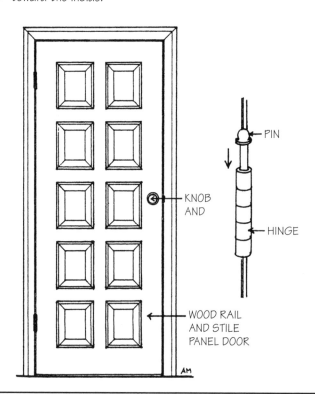

KNOB AND

PIN

HINGE

WOOD RAIL AND STILE PANEL DOOR

AM

5 Hang the door by aligning the hinge leaves and inserting the pins. Check for fit; plane edges if necessary.

6 Install the doorknob (with lock, if desired) so that the latch meets the striker plate.

Note: Weather-strip if the door opens to the outside.

FRENCH DOORS

The most critical aspect of hanging French or double doors is getting the jambs as perfectly parallel and level as possible.

1 Establish location and frame in door as shown; allow for door frame (usually 3½") plus ¹⁄₁₆" around the doors at the sides, top and in between, allow ½" at bottom.

2 Install sill, door frame, exterior and interior trim, and threshold.

3 Shim doors in place; mark doors and jambs for hinges, and mortise, using hinge leaves as templates; secure hinge leaves.

4 Hang doors by aligning hinge leaves to each other and inserting pins.

5 Mortise flush bolts into ends of one door; install knob and lock in the other.

6 Plane doors, if necessary; for smooth operation, apply finish to surfaces, weather-strip on all sides and at threshold.

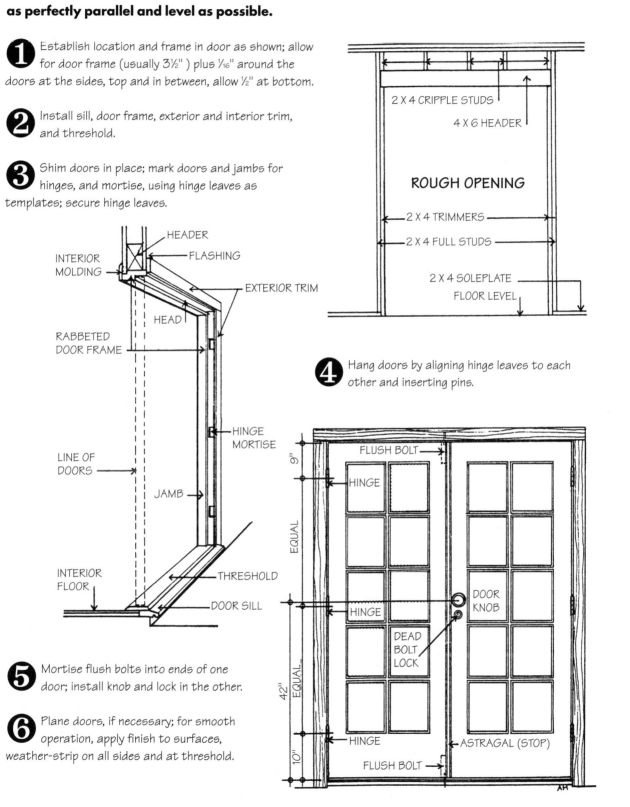

ROUGH OPENING

2 X 4 CRIPPLE STUDS
4 X 6 HEADER
2 X 4 TRIMMERS
2 X 4 FULL STUDS
2 X 4 SOLEPLATE
FLOOR LEVEL

HEADER
FLASHING
INTERIOR MOLDING
EXTERIOR TRIM
HEAD
RABBETED DOOR FRAME
HINGE MORTISE
LINE OF DOORS
JAMB
THRESHOLD
INTERIOR FLOOR
DOOR SILL

FLUSH BOLT
HINGE
9"
EQUAL
HINGE
DOOR KNOB
DEAD BOLT LOCK
42"
EQUAL
HINGE
ASTRAGAL (STOP)
10"
FLUSH BOLT

The frame usually comes with hinges attached and the doorstop molding tacked to the frame. Pull out the hinge pins, and remove the door before putting the frame in place.

For cutting a new door into an old wall, lay out the location and the measurement of the door. First, mark the line where the top of the new door header will meet the cut-off ends of old wall studs. This indicates the top line for cutting through wall coverings and determines where to cut the old studs. Figure this line by adding the header width plus ½ inch for shimming between the frame head jamb and the header; then add the door frame's height.

The sides, top and bottom of the rough opening for a door should be fitted with a strip of roofing felt or any other type of insulation to act as weather stripping.

The framing for a door must be absolutely square. Once the full-length studs are positioned, line up your trimmer studs' framing. Then install the header, usually a 4 × 4-inch piece of wood. Its length is the distance between the two existing full-length studs nearest the outside of each trimmer. Cut away the soleplate so it is flush with the full-length studs. Now figure the length of the trimmer studs; they extend from the floor to the base of the headers. Tack one trimmer against the inside of each full-length stud into the headers' ends, and toenail the cut-off, full-length studs into the top of the header. Nail the outer trimmers in place (into the studs).

To adjust the door frame to the proper width, place another trimmer out from one side parallel to the other trimmer stud and allow ½ inch on each side for shimming. Nail that trimmer into block; toenail to soleplate and headers. Use weather stripping on all sides and the threshold.

To replace a prehung frame within an existing opening, be sure the door frame is plumb and level at all times. (Follow Drawing 6-3 for this entire procedure.) The stud opening is somewhat larger than the size of the prehung frame to allow for shimming. To shim, drive shims into each side of the frame, between the trimmer studs and the jamb, to form a tight, rectangular wedge. After the frame is nailed in place, cut off the shim flush with the studs.

To position the door, center the frame in the opening from side to side and back to front; then shim the door to the estimated side clearance and fasten with stop moldings. Put shims next to the upper hinge, and tap them together so the side of the jamb is plumb. Shim, check the plumb, and nail halfway between top and bottom shims. Now fasten the door into position with hinge pins, and shim and nail the latch side of the door frame, always keeping a ¹⁄₁₆-inch clearance between the door edge and frame. Nail the door sill and threshold in place.

The doorknob and lock should be placed 36 to 38 inches above the floor. Drill for the knob and lock, carefully following the manufacturer's directions for attaching the lock. After the doorknob is secured, mark the top and bottom of the latch where it hits the frame. Position the latch's striker plate, and cut out the mortise for the latch.

The finishing touches are the doorstop molding and casing. Nail stops flush with the face of the closed door. Now nail casing trim around the opening to both the trimmer studs and the frame edges.

WINDOWS

Windows are the eyes of a house — you look out of them and people look into them — so windows deserve more thought than we give them. Just as you can tell a lot about people by their eyes, you also can tell a great deal about a house by its windows. Too often, windows were cold steel or aluminum stock-sized items installed where necessary without advance planning. But to make a house a home, windows should have character. I need cite only one prime example: In Drawing 6-4, notice the difference between the casement window and the standard aluminum sliding window. Which window has character? The casement, of course. Casement windows invariably add charm to a home because they break up the space into small units, which creates dimension and design. The eye has something to see rather than a blank stare. Select windows carefully; look for those with the character that can help, not hinder, the attitude of a house.

In addition to adding character, windows, of course, allow light and air to come into a room. Just where you place windows depends on your own personal preference — most people like a bright room, so they position windows accordingly, facing south or east. Some want a room that is somewhat dark, so windows are set on the north side (a bedroom would be an example). Also to be considered in window placement is climate. In cold climates, more windows should be oriented to the south to benefit from the heat of the sun. In mild climates, northern and eastern exposures avoid the heat of the sun.

Cross ventilation is a blessing in hot weather, so when placing windows, take into account this theory, which simply means air moving across the room. Before air conditioning, windows were the only source of ventilation, so if you want to save on energy and cost, it is wise to place windows where they will provide the best air circulation. For this purpose, upper walls and corners are not optimal positions. Locate windows that will take advantage of prevailing winds but not prevailing storms. (Heating costs will rise if you have a window wall where winter storms hit most frequently.)

In general, construct windows to relate to the character of the house, and place them to let the desired amount of air and light into the room.

RECESSED DOORS

Recessed doors present an alternative to building a porch roof over those '50s and '60s entryways that were constructed without concern for visitors.

ORIGINAL PLAN

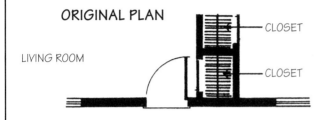

REMODELED

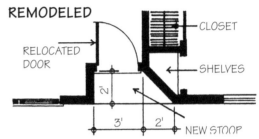

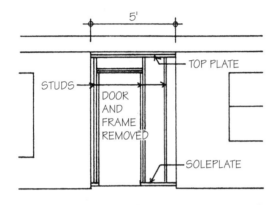

1 Remove the door, frame and wall siding to the desired width, then remove the studs and soleplate, but not the top plate.

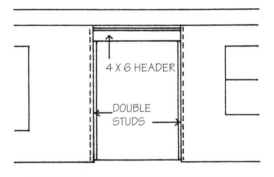

2 Insert 2 x 4 studs at the ends, then support the header with a second 2 x 4 at the ends; nail together.

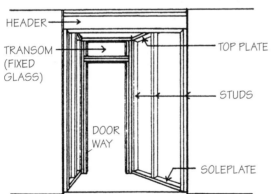

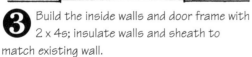

3 Build the inside walls and door frame with 2 x 4s; insulate walls and sheath to match existing wall.

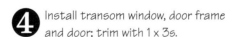

4 Install transom window, door frame and door; trim with 1 x 3s.

WINDOWS

The recent resurgence in window aesthetics has given the consumer a new realm of possibilities for curing their steel and aluminum window woes.

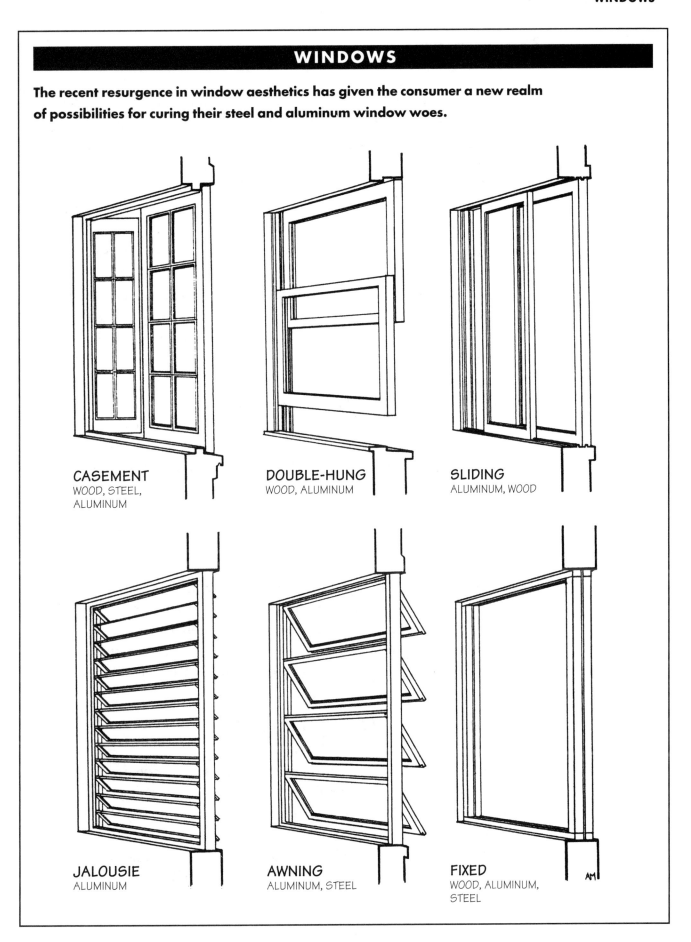

CASEMENT
WOOD, STEEL,
ALUMINUM

DOUBLE-HUNG
WOOD, ALUMINUM

SLIDING
ALUMINUM, WOOD

JALOUSIE
ALUMINUM

AWNING
ALUMINUM, STEEL

FIXED
WOOD, ALUMINUM,
STEEL

KINDS OF WINDOWS

There are actually hundreds of types of windows, and it sometimes is a dilemma to select the appropriate ones for a home. Generally, look for a window that has some character and will add to the tone of the house. I prefer a multipaned window. The small-pane effect is always attractive and fits into almost any home, from Victorian to contemporary. Sliding windows (horizontal sliders) seem sterile to me, and pivoting or hopper-type windows, although they have their uses, are not very handsome.

Fixed windows that do not open are often used in today's houses, and we will discuss these as well.

In most regions of the country, windows are bought ready-made (sometimes called *setup* windows). They come with *sash* (the frame that holds the glass); *jamb* (the top and side members); *casing* (the outside frame); and a *sill* (the bottom member).

Decide on the size and shape of the window first because the rough opening must be cut to accommodate the units. You can order windows almost any jamb thickness, but it must relate to the thickness of the wall. For example, most walls are made of 2 × 4 (3½ inches wide); ½″ sheathing (on the outside) and ½″ wallboard (on the inside). This totals 4½ inches, and if your house walls measure 4½ inches, your jambs can be no wider.

Casement Windows

Wood casement windows come in a variety of patterns, but the more panels of glass in a wall, the better effect it will have. The larger the span of casement windows, the more character; casement windows rarely look good singly or in a distance less than 8 feet wide, because it is the repeated pattern that gives the windows their personality. Casement windows are available in dozens of sizes.

Dormer and Double-Hung Windows

The dormer window, popular because of its handsome shape, is essentially a casement window enclosed in a dormer frame, giving a pleasing, shadow-box effect. The header and sill jut out, but the window itself is recessed; this provides both dimension and detailing.

The workhorse window of yesteryear was the double-hung window: two windows, one above the other, double hung. As a functional window, it cannot be beat.

Fixed Arched Window

An arched window is hard to find at suppliers, but occasionally you may find an old church window, as I did at a salvage outlet. I felt that the graceful curve of the window frame and the general attitude of the window itself would add character to the kitchen area, and it did. Thus, I am adding some details here about installing an arched window. If you use benderboard (which is available at lumberyards), you can do the window installation without too much trouble.

The installation of the arched window follows the same procedure as for any window. Install the header and the frame opening, allowing for the jamb thickness plus ⅛-inch space for the top and sides. Drawing 6-5 shows a typical fixed arched window installation.

Bay Windows

One bay window can add beauty to any plain home, and its construction, although somewhat more complicated than a standard window, is not overpowering. The bay window, like most other types of windows, can be purchased as a unit and comes complete with sash, jamb and casing, so much of the work is done for you. It is ready to insert into a rough-framed opening. You can also make your own bay window if you want something more distinctive and you don't mind a bit more work. The work is worth the effort because it results in a unique look.

To install a bay window, first determine the size and location of the bay. Then start the foundation work for the window; this requires a suitable concrete foundation that, if possible, should join the existing foundation of the house. A concrete footing is necessary to support the foundation. Check local building codes to determine the frost line and depth of the footing. Excavate and level the ground for the footing. Use rented forms from rent-it companies or build your own, and pour the footing and foundation. If you do not want to deal with concrete work, you can hire a professional to pour the concrete. (See Drawings 6-6 and 6-7.) Be sure to install necessary tie rods and reinforcing rods. When the concrete foundation is ready, you can remove the siding; cut the siding as wide as the outside dimension of the foundation wall and as high as the ceiling. Now remove the interior wall, the studs and the soleplate, but do not remove the top plate. Nail in place 2 × 4 full studs on each side running top to bottom between the soleplate and the top plate. Nail trimmer studs to the full studs; these support the header. Check local building codes for exact size of the header. Be sure to put in the cripple studs above the header to support the top plate.

A mudsill is necessary for the window, so use a 2 × 4 bolted to the foundation. Now remove the blocking at the existing floor joists and put in new joists as

FIXED ARCHED WINDOW

Any window shape can be fitted into a wall — from oval to round to geometric.

1 *See How to Replace a Window.* Raise header if necessary; frame the window area, allowing for the jamb thickness plus a ⅛" space at the sides and top.

2 Shim the window temporarily in place; nail diagonal 2 x 4s, again allowing for the jamb thickness plus ⅛".

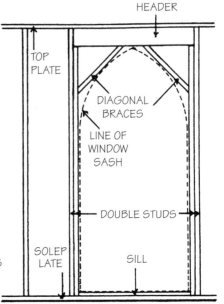

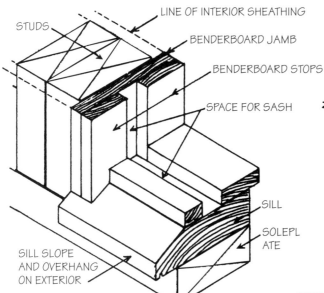

3 Measure and cut redwood benderboard jamb to fit between window sash and structural framing. Cut strips for interior and exterior stops, allowing for sash plus ⅛" for weatherseal (jamb should be flush with interior and exterior sheathing).

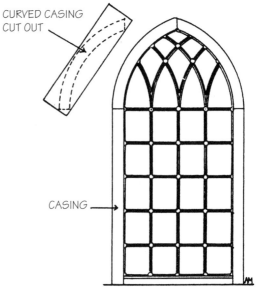

4 Attach the benderboard jamb to the framing and the exterior stops to the jamb. (Use caulk between pieces, and nail together.)

5 Install window, center sash with finishing nails, nail interior stops, and seal with silicone wetherseal.

6 Replace interior and exterior sheathing, insulate wall, and cut curved casings from 1" boards. Match to straight lower casings.

shown in step 4 of Drawing 6-6. Install the new plywood subfloor and a 2×4 soleplate at the outside edge.

It is now time to frame in the bay using 2×4 studs and trimmers; finish at the top with a double 2×4 top plate. To make the union with the house roof, install 2×4 rafters and ceiling joists; add a ledger on the house and the top plate. Match the exterior finish of the existing house wall, and finish the bay with siding that matches the house walls to complete the project.

Flashing and trimming are the final steps; the flashing is the metal stripping to prevent leaks, and the trim is standard molding. Install the windows as shown in Drawing 6-7; then do the painting and staining to match existing surfaces.

Installation

Let's suppose the present windows in your home just do not do anything for the building. Your home needs some character, and the old French doors you found would give that character if they were used as windows. How can you install the doors? Where should you place the doors for maximum effect? How do you replace any window? First, determine if the wall you want the windows on is load-bearing. Any exterior wall or interior one at right angles to the ceiling joists is usually considered a load-bearing wall. If the wall is load-bearing, then you will need to beef up your headers. Consult your local building department for requirements.

Now that you have the right wall, remove existing sash, frame, trim and interior wall sheathing. (Follow Drawing 6-8 for this discussion.) Add 3 inches, and set full-length studs here. Cut two 2×4s to measure the height of the rough opening. These studs support the header (generally two 2×6s nailed together with 16d nails for a 2-foot-wide window in a load-bearing wall). Use a spacer of $3/8''$ plywood to make the header equal to the width of a 2×4.

Nail the two full-length studs to the header; use 16d nails. The header itself is connected to the top plate by two 2×4s.

Occasionally, with different ceiling heights, the header fits snug against the bottom of the top plate, so no connecting studs are necessary. Headers are of the same size unless the window is extra wide.

If the window is 3 to 5 feet wide, use 2×8s; if the window is over 6 feet, use 2×10s; and so on. Nail a 2×4 between the supporting studs at the height of the bottom of the window's rough opening. Nail short studs on 16-inch centers, and support this crosspiece or sill of the rough opening. Toenail the sill to the supporting studs with 10d nails; face-nail the studs with 16d nails. Toenail the studs (or cripples) to the plate with 10d nails.

ADDING A BAY WINDOW

Adding a bay window is a big task, but the result is a dramatic addition to both the interior and the exterior of your home.

1 Establish the size and location of the bay on the interior and exterior. Pour a concrete foundation similar to the one existing, and tie into it with steel tie rods (consult local building codes).

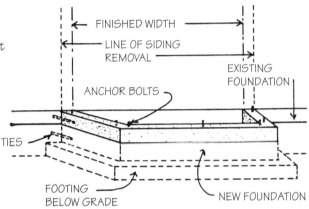

FINISHED WIDTH

LINE OF SIDING REMOVAL

ANCHOR BOLTS

EXISTING FOUNDATION

TIES

FOOTING BELOW GRADE

NEW FOUNDATION

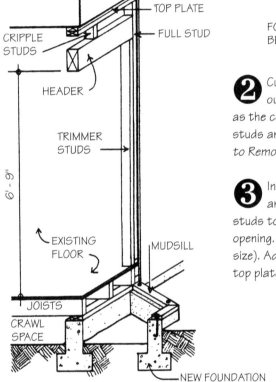

TOP PLATE

FULL STUD

CRIPPLE STUDS

HEADER

TRIMMER STUDS

6'-9"

EXISTING FLOOR

MUDSILL

JOISTS

CRAWL SPACE

NEW FOUNDATION

2 Cut and remove the siding as wide as the outside dimension of the foundation and as high as the ceiling. Remove the interior sheathing, the studs and soleplate, but not the top plate (see *How to Remove a Wall*).

3 Install 2 x 4 full-height studs between the sole and top plates. Nail with 2 x 4 x 6'-9" trimmer studs to support a header at both ends of the opening. Nail the header in place (consult codes for size). Add 2 x 4 cripple studs above, to support the top plate.

Note: The opening may be temporarily sealed with plywood sheets on the interior side.

4 Bolt a 2 x 4 redwood mudsill to the foundation, remove the blocking at the existing floor joists and attach new joists, overlapped 6", from the existing sill to the new sill. Add new blocking at the ends and provide air vents through the blocking, as required by the codes.

5 Nail a plywood subfloor so that the new floor level matches the existing floor (shim, if necessary). Then nail a 2 x 4 soleplate at the outside edge.

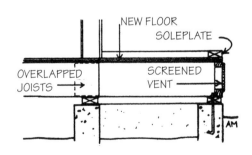

NEW FLOOR SOLEPLATE

OVERLAPPED JOISTS

SCREENED VENT

AM

If the poured concrete, full-length window seems like too big of a job, consider a boxed-in bay window that only extends downward to the top of the sill of your house.

6 Frame in the bay with 2 x 4 studs and trimmers to support the headers over the windows. Frame the windows, depending on the size. Finish at the top with a double 2 x 4 top plate. Attach the framing to the house with lag screws.

7 Frame the roof with 2 x 4 rafters and ceiling joists. Attach on a ledger at the house and the top plate. Sheath with ⅝" exterior plywood and roof similar to the house.

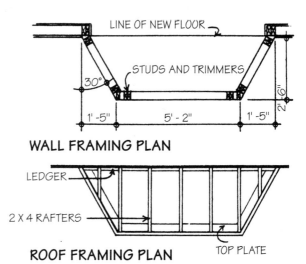

LINE OF NEW FLOOR

STUDS AND TRIMMERS

30°

1' -5"   5' - 2"   1' -5"

2'-6"

WALL FRAMING PLAN

LEDGER

2 X 4 RAFTERS

TOP PLATE

ROOF FRAMING PLAN

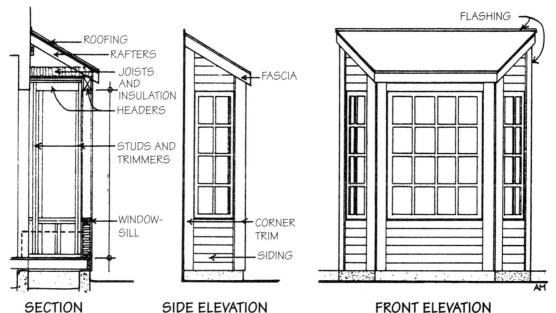

ROOFING
RAFTERS
JOISTS AND INSULATION
HEADERS
STUDS AND TRIMMERS
WINDOW-SILL

SECTION

FASCIA
CORNER TRIM
SIDING

SIDE ELEVATION

FLASHING

AM

FRONT ELEVATION

8 Enclose the bay with siding to match the house. Flash and trim at the corners, insulate the ceilings and walls (see *Insulating Ceilings* and *Insulating Walls*). Then sheath the interior walls and ceiling as desired, and install interior molding.

9 Install windows (see *How to Replace a Window*). Trim the window frames inside and out, paint and/or stain the interior and exterior surfaces and trim. Finish the floor to match the existing one, or install a fixed window seat.

HOW TO REPLACE A WINDOW

Window replacement looks like a formidable job when begin to count up all the windows in your house. Take it one or two windows at a time and you'll be able to do a better and more attractive job than the window replacement companies can offer.

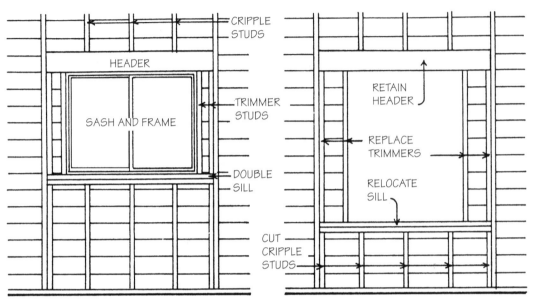

① Remove the sash, window frame, and trim and interior wall sheathing.

② Reframe opening; allow ⅜" on all sides of new window. Repair exterior siding.

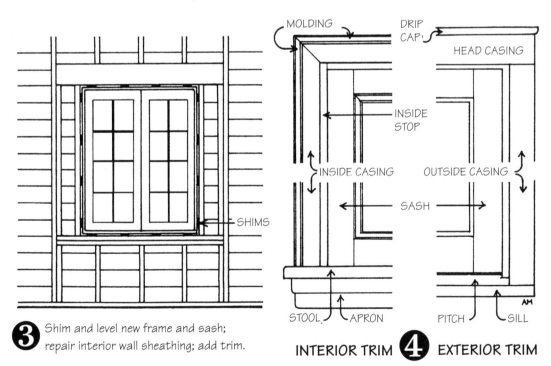

③ Shim and level new frame and sash; repair interior wall sheathing; add trim.

INTERIOR TRIM ④ EXTERIOR TRIM

WINDOW AND SHEET GLASS

In our remodeling we deal with *flat glass* — sheets of glass for windows and sky-lights. A little knowledge about glass can help you work better with it and know what to look for when shopping.

Flat glass comes in several thicknesses and qualities, much like lumber. Very thin glass is ¹⁄₆₄″ thick; very thick glass is 1″ thick. The glass we use in windows is ¹⁄₁₆″, ¹⁄₁₀″ or ⅛″ thick and comes in two grades: *A-glass*, with little or no flaws, and *B-glass* or commercial glass, which has some small marks or seeds — not exceeding ¹⁄₃₂″ long — in the glass.

Standard window glass (sold at hardware and glass stores) is an imperfect product. It is a rolled glass and inherently has flaws. That is, it is poured in a liquid state and sent through rollers to obtain its thickness and flatness. Window glass is called SSA and SSB (¹⁄₁₆″ thick) or DSA and DSB (⅛″ thick); it always contains some waves because it has gone through a roller process.

Window glass comes in boxes of 50 or 100 square feet, in sizes from 8″ × 10″ to 36″ × 60″. Glass is priced on the even inch, and since you do not want too many sheets, you will probably buy glass by the piece. It pays to buy stock sizes (even inch) rather than having it cut to a specific size of say 8½″ × 10¼″ (unless a specific size is necessary) because you would pay for 10″ × 12″.

The glass you buy will have clean-cut edges, with no protection against sharpness. You can specify glass with seamed or ground edges so the sharpness will be removed.

Also available is *crystal glass*, which designates glass ³⁄₁₆″ and ⁷⁄₃₂″ thick. The heavier the glass, the less apt it is to break, and for some panels, the heavier glass is a wise choice. Crystal glass is more expensive than window glass, but small pieces, say 10″ × 20″, are relatively inexpensive.

Polished Plate Glass

Polished plate glass is essentially glass polished on both surfaces by huge buffer wheels so all waviness is eliminated. This glass is more costly than window and sheet glass, but it is perfect if you want a very fine window. Polished plate glass is available in ⅛″ and ¼″ thicknesses. As with other glass, it should be ordered on the even inch, with all edges seamed or ground.

Thermal Glass

You can also buy insulating glass known in the trade as *double-pane* (or as Thermopane or Dual Glaze, among other trade names). This type of glass is constructed of two pieces of glass sealed in a vacuum and bonded at all edges. This window unit reduces noise and cuts down on energy costs. Combined with Low E glass, the double-glazed window is a formidable energy saver. *Low E* means low emissivity; the *E* designates a thin layer of oxide coating on the glass. It is said to stop some ultraviolet radiation, and thus reduces fading of interior objects. Bronze glass and gray glass are other types of glass designed to cut down glare and radiation.

Stained Glass

Stained glass is also called *cathedral glass* or *antique glass* in the trade. It is translucent, colored glass, with ripples or mounds on one surface and the other surface smooth, or with both surfaces textured. Cathedral glass is slightly thicker than standard SSB window glass and is cut in the same manner as window glass. This glass costs much more than clear glass; it is sold at glass stores and craft shops.

Cutting Glass

Cutting glass with a glass cutter is actually a simple process if you score or fracture the glass only when making the cut. The fracture causes the glass molecules to separate along the line being scored. The secret of using the glass cutter (available inexpensively at hardware stores) is the amount of pressure applied. The pressure must be uniformly applied and neither too heavy nor too light. The next important trick is to break the glass immediately before the separated molecules heal themselves.

To actually break the glass, place a long pencil or strip of wood underneath the score line. Then press down with the palms of each hand, one palm on each side of the cut, to apply enough (but not too much) pressure. The impact of the palms on the glass breaks it along a clean-cut line.

Be sure the glass is clean; wash it with detergent, rinse it with warm water and dry thoroughly. Set the glass pane on a level table protected with an old carpet or bath towel. Hold the cutter almost perpendicular and dip it into oil; get a small dab of oil on the cutting wheel. For a straight cut, use a guide such as a yardstick. Start about 1/32 inch from the end edge of the glass (to avoid edge chipping), and make a firm, continuous cut without lifting the cutter. You will know if you are doing it properly because the cutter on the glass makes a smooth and even sound. As soon as the glass is scored, place the wooden pencil directly under the score line, and immediately place your thumbs or palms on each side of the line. Apply pressure; the glass will separate. If the glass does not break, use the end of the cutter and tap gently along the scored line. You should see a fracture develop along the line. Then apply equal pressure to the two sides of the fracture line and snap the glass apart.

Shaped pieces of glass—curves, arcs—require more expertise. For these, cardboard patterns are necessary: Place them on the glass, then apply the score line as you would for straight cuts. To separate a thin glass strip from a wider piece, use glass pliers. (Glass pliers are simply pliers that have been detempered. You can make your own glass pliers by heating the jaws until red hot, and then allowing them to cool without quenching.) Grasp the narrow side of the glass with the pliers and the other side with your hand, and snap off the small piece with the pliers. Corners or slight projections can be nipped off with the indented part of the glass cutter or with flat-nosed pliers.

No matter what kind of glass you are using or what kind of cut is being made, you must follow certain safety precautions. Sharp edges of glass will cut you, so wear an old pair of household gloves and safety goggles. Avoid grasping or holding glass by its edges; doing so will cause you to be cut. Always keep your body and feet at a safe distance from the cutting table, and never cut glass close to your face.

The thinner the glass, the easier it is to cut. If you are cutting glass $\frac{3}{16}''$ or $\frac{1}{4}''$ thick, do it only after you have experience in glass cutting. And if the idea of cutting glass frightens you altogether (although it should not), try some practice cuts on scraps first; otherwise, buy glass already cut at stores.

CHAPTER SEVEN

WALLS

I f you are remodeling a house, you will find that there is always a wall, which, if removed, would open up two areas and double the space both visually and physically. Whether you remove the wall completely (which is OK if the wall is not load-bearing) or remove the wall and replace it with charming posts or pilasters, you open a whole new dimension in a house. If you want to be even more ornamental, and if the house demands it, you might think about archways — an old-fashioned feature that makes a home inviting.

CONSTRUCTION LANGUAGE

BASEBOARD: A milled board nailed onto the wall at floor line.

BLOCKING: A wooden block used as a temporary support.

BRACE: A board set at an angle.

CORNER BEAD: A piece of wood with an indentation on each side for protecting angle of wall.

COUNTERSINK: To set the head of a screw or nail at or below the surface.

DOUBLE HEADER: Door or window lintel made from two pieces of lumber, placed upright and nailed together.

DOUBLE STUDS: Double vertical supports.

GUSSET: A board connecting rafters butting end to end.

LINTEL: A horizontal piece of wood that supports an opening for a door or window.

METAL LATHING: A grid-pattern metal sheet.

POLYETHYLENE VAPOR BARRIER: Plastic sheets used to prevent moisture absorption.

SHIPLAP: A board with a groove to allow each board to overlap the other but with surfaces on the same plane.

SOLEPLATE: A bottom horizontal board, usually 2×6, at floor line.

TONGUE AND GROOVE: A board with a tongue in one edge and a groove in the other.

TOP PLATE: Horizontal board doubled, usually a 2×6 above door and window opening.

WING WALL: A wall built at a right angle.

REMOVING A WALL

It is tougher to remove a wall than to put up the columns or posts — so be prepared to use some muscle. First, determine whether the wall is load-bearing. Any exterior or interior wall that is at right angles to the ceiling joists is usually considered a bearing wall. When you remove a wall, you must install a suitable header to hold the weight of the roof above it; an opening width of 4 to 6 feet requires a 4×6 header; a 6- to 8-foot opening requires a 4×8 header; and a 10-foot opening requires a 4×10 header. A width of more than 10 feet increases the size of the necessary header to 4 × 14. Since you will be handling large header timbers, get some help from friends or relatives; and order the header at least 2 feet longer than the length of the opening. (You can trim the header after determining the exact stud spacing.) Once the wall is removed, you will need supports while you ready the window opening, posts or other structural elements. Use floor jacks (see Drawing 7-2) or temporary bracing to hold the wall while work is in progress.

Look at Drawings 7-1 and 7-2, which show how to remove a bearing wall and a nonbearing wall, respectively. Removing a wall is not an insurmountable task if you do it easily and slowly. To get the opening started, use a power or keyhole saw to cut into the wall where you want the opening; when the opening is large enough, use a crosscut saw. If the wall is lath board, you can saw without too much damage to surrounding surfaces. Expose enough of the framing so you can install a new header and trimmer studs. Remove the wall with a crowbar, or if the opening is small, use the claw end of a rip hammer, prying gently but firmly.

If the wall is plaster, use the claw end of the hammer to chop out a horizontal ribbon of plaster between two laths as close as possible to the outline of the desired opening. Then, with a cold chisel and hammer, chop away 4 to 6 inches of plaster inside the vertical lines to expose the lathing. Saw through the lathing as closely as possible to a stud.

If you are removing an exterior wall for a new window opening, you might run into stucco-and-wire construction. Here you must use muscle power and smash the stucco with a hammer or hatchet to expose the chicken wire; cut the wire with tin snips, then pull away the old sections from the sheathing. The easiest way to approach the stucco exterior wall is to use a power masonry saw, which allows you to saw through the stucco and wire at the same time. Wear leather gloves and protective goggles for this project.

If the exterior wall is wood siding, all you need is a power saw and hammer. In most cases, wall repairing will entail installing new studs or replastering to seal and cover your tear-out. These are not difficult jobs; in fact, the patch-up is fun. Patch up with wood, plaster, or whatever the situation calls for. With wood, just cut out replacement pieces the size of the area to be covered, nail the pieces into place, and finish with a molding. With plaster, build up the surface of the torn opening a little at a time and smooth the plaster.

PLASTER

Most older buildings have plaster applied over strips of horizontally attached wood on the wall framing. The plaster (actually, the base coat is more like

HOW TO REMOVE A WALL

Dealing with load-bearing walls is not a job beyond amateur skills. Patience and good preplanning make the job a simple matter of ordinary carpentry.

1 Determine whether the wall is load-bearing or nonbearing.

A. If the ceiling joists are at right angles to the wall, the wall is supporting the ceiling joists and is load-bearing. The wall will have to be replaced with a supporting beam and posts at both ends.

B. If the ceiling joists are parallel to the wall and if there isn't a wall directly above on a second floor, the wall is nonbearing and can be safely removed.

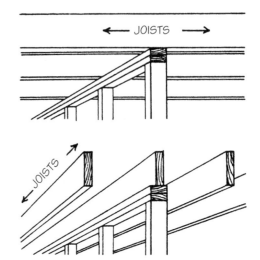

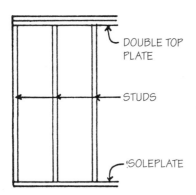

DOUBLE TOP PLATE

STUDS

!SOLEPLATE

2 Remove any doors, all molding and the wall sheathing on both sides. Relocate any electrical wiring.

3 If the wall is nonbearing, remove the studs, soleplate and top plate. Patch the walls, ceiling and floor to match the existing surfaces.

4 If the wall is load-bearing, consult local building codes for the size of the beam required to support the ceiling joists. Build temporary supporting walls 3' from each side of the wall to be removed, using 2 x 4 studs 24" on center, a 2 x 4 soleplate and top plate.

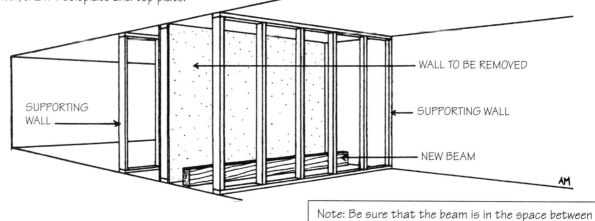

SUPPORTING WALL

WALL TO BE REMOVED

SUPPORTING WALL

NEW BEAM

AM

Note: Be sure that the beam is in the space between the supporting walls before building them.

5 Remove the bearing-wall studs, top plate and soleplate. Then carefully measure the height from the floor to the bottom of the joists. Cut two 4 x 4 posts, deducting the height of the beam.

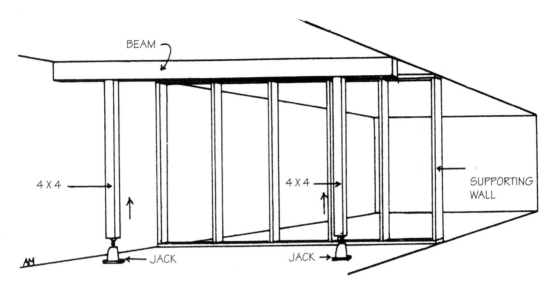

BEAM

4 X 4

4 X 4

SUPPORTING WALL

JACK

JACK

6 Support the new beam in place with two 4 x 4s on top of house jacks. Carefully align the beam and raise it slightly so that the permanent 4 x 4 posts can be placed under each end.

7 Attach the posts to the walls with lag screws or by toenailing. In either case, countersink them and fill the holes with wood putty.

8 Lower the beam in place. Remove the 4 x 4s and the jacks. Toenail the beam to the posts. Then remove the temporary supporting walls.

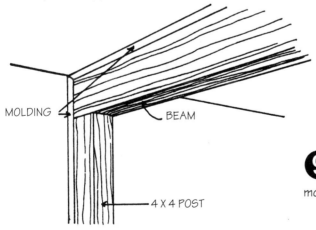

MOLDING

BEAM

4 X 4 POST

9 Countersink the nails and fill with wood putty. Patch the floor and walls as required. Add molding and finish with stain or paint as desired.

concrete) was applied over the lath. Another method used is to apply plaster directly over sheets of gypsum board (known as rock lath). The plaster applied may be done in various finishes depending on the desired effect—smooth, mottled, swirled, sponged or "stomped." The latter is achieved with a large, round brush made for that purpose.

Plastering techniques are true skills. You can do it, but you may have to practice first in order to get a feel for the material.

WOOD PANELING

Wood paneling is available in many finishes in standard prefinished sheets and various types of veneer. Shop first before making a decision. The paneled wall usually lends itself to a library, a guest room, or some room that is not too large. Too much paneling (contrary to what manufacturers say) can make a room confining.

To panel a wall, as shown in Drawing 7-3, first remove the baseboard and any moldings and trim at doors and windows. In other words, strip off the existing materials. If the wall is masonry or uneven, you must fur it out with strips. Attach wood panels with adhesive or nails; the basic installation is simple once the preparation is done. When the paneling is finished, attach all moldings and trim.

DIAGONAL SIDING

Today, you can perform miracles with surface wall treatment, an application of siding or board. Siding is generally ¾" thick, varying from 3⅛" to 10¹³⁄₁₆" wide. (The actual dimensions of your walls will dictate the width of the siding.) Small rooms should be done in narrow siding, 3⅛"; larger areas benefit from wide siding.

Remove any existing wall covering, and prepare the wall for the siding. When you apply siding, it is imperative that you start right. Begin at a lower corner with a perfect 45° angle; nail each board to studs. The last piece of wood must be pattern-cut into place as shown in Drawing 7-4.

If you are using tongue-and-groove, the first piece at the triangle should be tongue up. If you are using shiplap, the upper lap should be up. In tongue-and-groove construction, the last piece must have the tongue removed for flush fitting.

If you have done the construction properly and all is even and flush, base-

WOOD PANELED WALL

The primary aim in insulating is to stop the flow of air through walls and ceilings. Don't forget to check your basement and attic spaces for openings to wall cavities.

Note: Paneling is available in 4' x 8' or 4' x 10' prefinished sheets and various types of grooved or plain plywood (such as rough sawn or fine veneers).

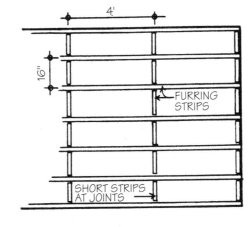

1 Remove the baseboard, any molding and trim at doors and windows, etc.

2 If the wall is masonry or is uneven, attach 1 x 2 furring strips horizontally at 16" on center (use masonry nails). If dampness is a problem, staple a polyethylene vapor barrier to the furring strips.

3 Move any electrical boxes out to be flush with the new wall surface.

4 Measure the wall height at several points, and cut the panels about ¼" less than the measurement.

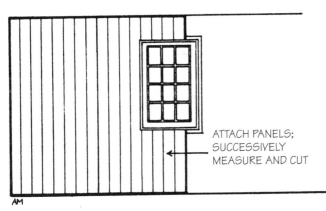

ATTACH PANELS; SUCCESSIVELY MEASURE AND CUT

5 Carefully measure and cut openings for windows, doors and electrical outlets. Use a saber saw or a coping saw.

6 The panels can be attached with adhesive and/or nails. Apply the adhesive with either a caulking gun or with a notched trowel (follow manufacturer's directions). Nails to match paneling are available, or countersink finishing nails and fill with matching wood putty.

7 Attach matching molding or refinish the existing molding and reinstall. Countersink nails and fill with matching wood putty.

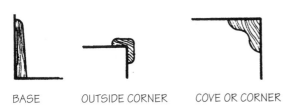

BASE   OUTSIDE CORNER   COVE OR CORNER

DIAGONAL SIDING

Don't skimp on paneling. If a job takes twenty sheets of paneling, your decision to save five dollars per sheet on a cheaper product may not make you happy when all the work is done.

1 Start at a lower corner with a 45° triangle (other angles may be used). If tongue-and-groove, the tongue should be up; if shiplap, the underlap should be up.

2 Carefully measure and cut each successive board with ends at 45°. Nail to studs with finishing nails. Be sure to move any electrical boxes out to be flush with the new wall surface.

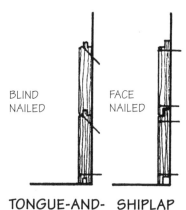

BLIND NAILED   FACE NAILED

TONGUE-AND-GROOVE   SHIPLAP

Note: Siding is usually ¾" thick and varies from 3⅛" to 10¹³⁄₁₆" wide. Tongue-and-groove can be blind nailed (concealed). Shiplap or other joints must be face nailed.

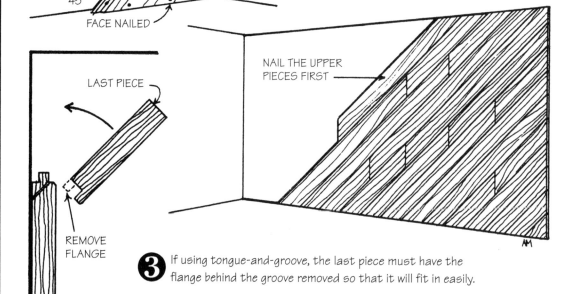

45°

FIRST PIECE

BLIND NAIL AT TONGUE

45°   90°

FACE NAILED

LAST PIECE

REMOVE FLANGE

NAIL THE UPPER PIECES FIRST

3 If using tongue-and-groove, the last piece must have the flange behind the groove removed so that it will fit in easily.

4 The wood can be stained (follow manufacturer's directions) or left natural. In either case, apply a clear finish.

5 Baseboard and trim are not necessary when the boards have been evenly installed. Countersink the nails and fill with matching putty.

board and trim should not be used because they detract from the total pattern. However, if the construction is not perfect, use trim to cover errors.

INSULATING WALLS

Insulating a wall is really an easy process. In fact, it is so easy that it is usually overlooked; but insulation saves heat in the winter and keeps houses cool in the summer. Generally, only exterior walls are insulated. Insulation (and there are several types available, of which the aluminum foil rock wool is the most popular) involves placing the insulation padding within the studs and stapling it in place. Always install fiberglass insulation with the papered or foiled side toward the living area. If loose-fill insulation is used, it is generally blown into place. If your walls are masonry, apply board or sheet insulation to the interior side, and then apply wall finish over the insulation.

Drawing 7-5 contains insulation data. Always check local building codes for the minimum amount of insulation required.

INSULATING WALLS

Diagonal siding gives a home a modern, progressive or intelligent air without seeming trendy and dated. Diagonals at 45° are the most visually successful and the easiest to lay out.

Note: Usually only the perimeter (exterior) walls are insulated, but insulating interior partitions can help to control sound.

1 If the studs are accessible from the interior (before the wall sheathing is applied), staple batts or blankets between the studs.

2 If the studs are sheathed and the wall can be drilled into, have loose fill professionally blown in.

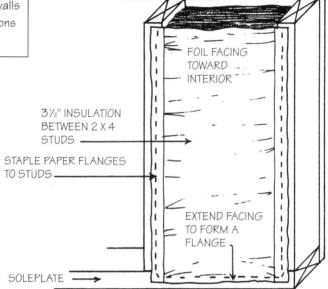

FOIL FACING TOWARD INTERIOR

3½" INSULATION BETWEEN 2 X 4 STUDS

STAPLE PAPER FLANGES TO STUDS

EXTEND FACING TO FORM A FLANGE

SOLEPLATE

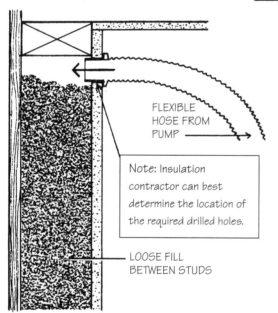

FLEXIBLE HOSE FROM PUMP

Note: Insulation contractor can best determine the location of the required drilled holes.

LOOSE FILL BETWEEN STUDS

Note: Check local building codes for the minimum amount of insulation required.

3 If the walls are solid (masonry), apply board or sheet insulation to the interior side and apply wall finish over.

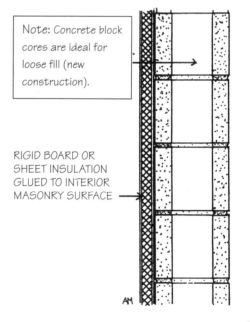

Note: Concrete block cores are ideal for loose fill (new construction).

RIGID BOARD OR SHEET INSULATION GLUED TO INTERIOR MASONRY SURFACE

CHAPTER EIGHT

SKYLIGHTS

For many years, solid, bleak ceilings covered our house and apartment worlds. The skylight, once used only in factory ceilings, is now popular for our living needs—and rightly so. Skylights can add more light, grace and beauty, as well as a feeling of spaciousness, to a room than any other building device. So what took them so long to become popular? Until recently, there were few skylight kits available to the public (the plastic bubble skylight kit was perhaps the first one introduced), and glass skylights used to leak (although today there are excellent sealers available).

Besides being bubble shaped, skylights can be flat, recessed, flush, hipped, gable or triangular; they can be built of plastic, Plexiglas, glass or other materials. Skylights can go into almost any roofed room in the home, but they are dramatically outstanding in living rooms and in bathrooms. Whether the room has a high or a low ceiling, a skylight will create a distinctive effect: the low-ceilinged room will seem taller, and the high-ceilinged one, more dimensional and less barren. So put skylights wherever you want light and beauty. The material and design of the skylight—no matter what room the skylight is in—is of utmost importance, so for aesthetic purposes, I recommend using glass and wood. Glass is heavier than plastic but does not discolor or mar as either acrylic or plastic tends to do.

As a structural device, the skylight requires good framing and flashing where it joins the roof to avoid leakage.

CONSTRUCTION LANGUAGE

CANT STRIP: An angled strip installed on 2 × 6 curbs.
CAULKING: Flexible material used to seal seams and joints.
SILICONE SEALANT: A special compound sealant for joints.
STRUTS: 2 × 2 pieces of wood that support glazing.

SKYLIGHTS

Years ago, skylights were difficult to install, and they always leaked. The units were made of wire glass or tempered glass; tempered glass skylights are still available, but they are very expensive. However, today's new materials — even better than tempered glass — and the new methods of installation are the keys to an attractive, light-filled room. Skylights are available in many shapes and sizes: No longer are they restricted to the bubbles and domes of the past. If you want a glass skylight, you can select from bronze or gray tints, with light-reflecting coatings. But even better are skylights made from the rigid and durable plastics that can be shaped into various designs and do not yellow with age. These plastics are also available with gray or white solar tints. Skylights are sold ready-made in stock sizes.

Among many fine plastics, those made of Plexiglas are usually recommended for durability and long life. These acrylic skylights are .125-mil thick and are sold colorless, in bronze or dark bronze, gray or dark gray, and white or coated white. Colorless acrylic is used where maximum light is needed. White improves diffusion, and it lessens glare and heat. Bronze reduces glare and is aesthetically pleasing. Lexan seems to be the best Plexiglas on the market. Note that plastic is combustible and will burn if exposed to sufficient flame or fire.

Among the shapes you can select from in the ready-made skylights are domes, pyramids, octagons, pentagons and hexagons. Skylights are sold in single- or double-thickness construction; the double type is used when maximum energy conservation is desired. The three main types of skylights are:

1. conventional
2. automatic opening and closing
3. roof window

Some units are framed in wood, but most are framed in metal (curb-mounted); the metal is cut from extruded aluminum and welded at the corners for strength and durability. Framing is necessary for installation; these units are nailed or screwed over framed roof openings, and then the skylight is slotted into position and flashed and caulked. The units weather well, generally do not discolor, and resist damage from any impact.

Clean acrylic units with a solution of mild soap and lukewarm water. Swab the skylight with a clean cloth and then remove the excess solution with a clean cloth. Avoid window-cleaning products or scouring compounds, as they will scratch the plastic. Use naphtha or kerosene to remove tar or bird droppings.

OPENING THE ROOF

Installing a skylight requires removal of part of the roof and suitable rough framing, as previously explained. The toughest part of skylight installation is

SKYLIGHT DESIGNS — PLASTIC

Skylight manufacture has come a long way in the last ten to twenty years. With so many options available there is no longer any sense in building your own.

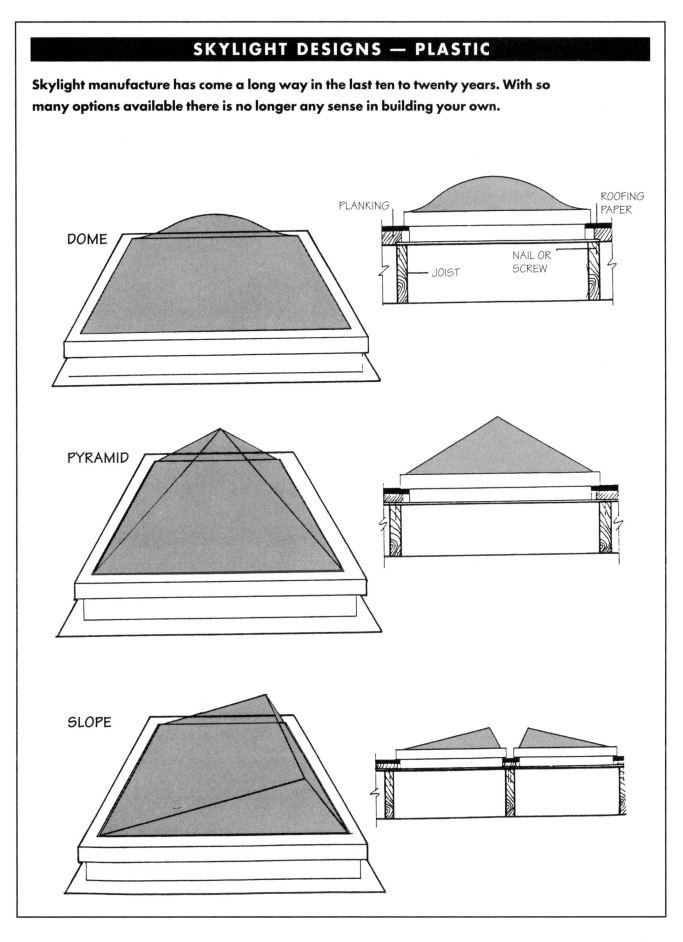

DOME

PLANKING

ROOFING PAPER

JOIST

NAIL OR SCREW

PYRAMID

SLOPE

cutting the hole or space for it. Use the reciprocating saw. The actual construction, as you can see from our drawings, is not difficult. Locate the skylight on the ceiling so you will have to cut a minimum number of joists. This involves working on a ladder and using a pry bar to remove existing roofing and ceiling materials. The mess is generally considerable, so have suitable tarps on the floor. Cut the hole in the ceiling or roof with a saw. To do this, drill holes at each corner and start the cut with a keyhole saw. Once the initial cut is made, a pry bar can be used to remove roofing or ceiling material. Then joists have to be cut and roof sheathing removed. Always cut away an additional 1½″ strip of roofing around the opening for installing the curb.

THE SKYLIGHT OPENING

For skylight work, you need a header, flashing, a curb, cement, glazing compounds and nails. No matter what kind of skylight you use, you will have to have a curb for it; a curb is the wood frame and is made of 2 × 6 lumber. Use highest-quality redwood because the skylight frame must be straight and aligned properly to avoid leaks.

Before you go cutting holes in your roof, examine the new skylight closely and be sure that you understand the way it will fit and how to frame for it. To put a skylight into an existing ceiling, place it so only a minimum number of joists will have to be cut. Cut through the ceiling, allowing for the header, which supports the cut joists. Now cut the joists and install the double headers (same size as the joists) on either side of the joists. Cut through the roof sheathing and roofing, and leave a 1½″ strip for the curb to fit into. Build the curb with 2 × 6s, with the same interior dimensions as the opening. Be sure the opening is square, or you will have quite a job installing the skylight. Now, as shown in step 5 of Drawing 8-2, pry roofing up around the edges, slide flashing into place and apply roof cement. Put the flashing in on all sides, and overlap it. Toenail the curb into place, and nail the flashing to the top edge of the curb. Finally, apply roof cement to the junction between the roofing and flashing.

The opening is now ready for a prefabricated skylight.

PREFABRICATED SKYLIGHTS

Prefabricated plastic bubbles or flat skylights are ready to slip into a curb (the curb consists of 2 × 6 boards nailed at the corners and fitted into the roof). The outer perimeter of the box skylight is usually made of aluminum and has merely

OPENING FOR A SKYLIGHT

Opening a roof can be both exciting and scary. Make sure you've got all your materials on hand and at least a two-day, good weather forecast.

1 Verify the dimensions. Locate the skylight on the ceiling so that a minimum number of joists will have to be cut. Cut through the ceiling, allowing for the headers (which support the cut joists).

2 Cut the joists and install the double headers (same size as the joists) on either side.

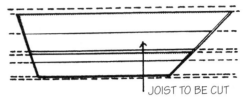

JOIST TO BE CUT

CEILING CUT AWAY (UNDERSIDE VIEW)

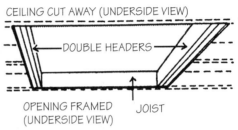

DOUBLE HEADERS

OPENING FRAMED (UNDERSIDE VIEW)   JOIST

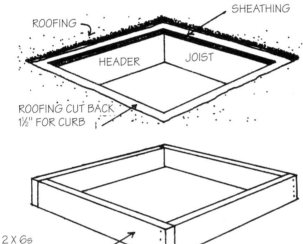

ROOF SHEATHING

ROOFING

HEADER   JOIST

ROOFING CUT BACK 1½" FOR CURB

2 X 6s GLUED AND NAILED

3 Cut through the roof sheathing and roofing, plus a 1½" strip of roofing around for setting the curb.

4 Build a curb with 2 x 6s with the same interior dimensions as the opening. Make sure that the corners are square (check skylight fit).

5 Pry roofing up around the edges. Apply roof cement and slide flashing in on all sides (overlap flashing).

6 Set the curb and toenail in place. Nail the flashing to the top edge of the curb.

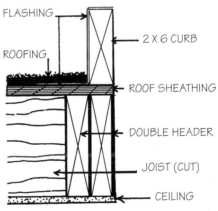

FLASHING

ROOFING

2 X 6 CURB

ROOF SHEATHING

DOUBLE HEADER

JOIST (CUT)

CEILING

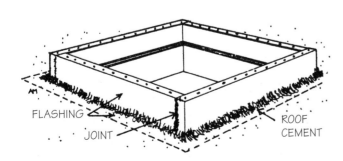

FLASHING

JOINT

ROOF CEMENT

7 Apply roof cement liberally to the junction of the roofing and flashing — also to the flashing joints.

to be slipped over the wooden curb and attached with nonhardening silicon.

To make the skylight completely leakproof, add flashing. Put the flashing strips in place on the roof, curve them against the curb, and then set the box skylight in place with appropriate adhesive. You can use single or double domes. The latter affords better insulation.

CHAPTER NINE

CEILINGS

A ceiling need not be a flat, confining surface; with some imagination it can be an integral part of the room's design. For example, exposed rafters and grid ceilings have a certain character, a charm that the more ordinary acoustical tile surfaces just do not have. Ceilings thus should be decorative as well as functional; alterations can be done easily.

CONSTRUCTION

In this book, we are concerned with remodeling details such as open ceilings with beams and rafters, rather than with the actual construction of a roof. However, a basic primer of roof construction will help you understand just how everything goes together.

CONSTRUCTION LANGUAGE

BOX BEAM: A beam made from three pieces of wood nailed together.

CHAMFER: An angled edge cut in wood.

COLLAR BEAMS: Two-inch boards connecting opposite roof rafters.

DRYWALL: Plasterboard in sheets for interior walls.

GYPSUM BOARD: A type of plasterboard.

JOINT COMPOUND: Plasterlike material to cover joint tape and nail holes.

PURLIN: A horizontal member of a roof supporting rafter.

RAFTER: A beam that supports the roof.

SPACKLE: Pastelike plaster material for repairing cracks.

TIE BEAMS: Beams that act as a tie roof.

TOGGLE BOLTS: Metal bolts for plaster walls.

TRUSS: A set of rafters connecting opposite wall points.

ROOFS

A ceiling (or roof—it might be one and the same, depending on how you look at it) is made up of joists and rafters. (A ceiling can be called the bottom of an upstairs bedroom or the bottom of a roof.) The rafters are set at an angle, reaching from a top ridge plate (the midrib of the skeleton). Ceiling joists (often 2 × 8s) are placed the width of the roof, two joists spanning the distance from the top plate of the second floor wall to the other wall. Joists are overlapped in the center where a bearing wall occurs.

The ceiling joists are cut at an angle at their ends so they can rest on the rafters and attach easily. Framing the roof is not very difficult, as you will see from our drawings, but the particular style of the roof affects the inside design. A building can have a pitched roof, hipped roof, gambrel roof, dormer roof, shed roof, and so on. The construction of these roofs is covered thoroughly in any number of books on home construction; let us briefly consider the designs themselves. The house's roof is really the frame of a structure, and as such creates a mood. The roof can be simple or ornate, formal or picturesque, utilitarian or decorative, or a little bit of each. The roofs of the Roman, classical and Renaissance periods were quite simple, usually flat, and played only a small part in the total appearance of the buildings. On the other hand, the historic French, Flemish and German roofs were high and steep, decorative, and enhanced with complex dormers and crowns. Without a doubt, the more complex roofs—dormer, gabled, mansard—have the crafted touch, but even the flat roof has its uses.

The *flat* roof is simple, clean, and, for wooden construction, presupposes a light load with short spans or permits a heavy load supported with columns and beams (quite handsome). But without a professional job done on its surface, it *will* leak.

The *pitched* roof has two slopes meeting at a ridge parallel to the long axis of the building and triangular gables at the ends.

The *hipped*, or *four-sloped*, roof consists of slopes equal to each other in pitch; the slopes form hips or intersections bisected by corners and terminate with a ridge or apex at the top.

The *mansard* roof has all sides divided into two slopes, the lower of which is steeper than the upper. This is a very decorative and ornate roof.

The *gambrel* roof is similar to the mansard and is built in the same way. It, too, is decorative and picturesque.

The popular and effective *gable* roof is easy to construct; it is basically triangular in shape.

The roof outlines your house; thus, it deserves consideration if you want a distinctive dwelling.

CEILINGS

Ceilings are flat or slightly curved, plain, beamed or coffered, depending on the materials used and the style of architecture. The *flat* treatment is perhaps the least effective but the most used; the addition of crown molding or a cornice where the walls meet the ceiling can give an unusual look to a flat ceiling and break the monotony of a plain, clean line. Another way to liven up a flat ceiling is to make it planked. A *planked* ceiling (usually called *tongue-in-groove*) consists of interlocking boards. The boards give a flat ceiling a texture and create a pleasant effect. Finally, you can eliminate much of the blandness of a flat ceiling by using various ceiling tiles.

The dramatic *beamed* ceiling is typical of many Renaissance and Gothic structures. Usually the larger beams of wood span the shorter dimension of the room, and the smaller ones are placed at right angles. The beamed ceiling is rigid in construction but flexible in decoration: The beams can be stained, carved or painted, and the patterns of the beams can vary considerably, each pattern lending a different quality to a room.

The *open-timbered* ceiling—an English creation—is really another treatment of the beamed ceiling of the Middle Ages. This ceiling is decorative, less complex than the standard beamed ceiling, and is quite effective because the open pattern, like the beamed ceiling, adds dimension and beauty to an area. However, the open-timbered ceiling is not quite as dramatic as the beamed ceiling.

The *coffered* ceiling has a very complex structure but a stellar look. The ceiling is divided into deep compartments of any desired shape, creating a dimensional look. The effect is highly dramatic, somewhat theatrical.

Gypsum board can be a suitable alternative to texture on a ceiling. It is easier and cheaper to apply, and its resistance to shock is especially useful in earthquake-prone areas.

Plaster ceilings can be damaged by excessive moisture, leaks in the roof and so on. To repair areas:

1. Remove loose plaster.
2. Undercut and enlarge hairline cracks to provide a base for the new material to adhere.
3. Dampen the crack and area around it; use a small, clean paintbrush dipped in water.
4. For small cracks, use vinyl spackling compound of board cement. Use a small, thin-bladed putty knife, and press material into the crack to fill it entirely.
5. Feather out (draw out and blend into the old plaster with the putty knife).
6. Allow repair to dry 24 hours.
7. Sand smooth with fine sandpaper wrapped on block.

You can also make designs in a standard painted plaster ceiling by using a wallpaper brush or other brush to create swirls, lines and so forth. Use a stipple-textured paint for best results.

RAFTERS AND BEAMS

The rafters and beams are the members that hold up the roof or the ceiling. Standard joist construction is used for most ceiling work. Exposing the joists and rafters adds depth and height to a room and imparts a totally different feeling than, say, a flat ceiling. Rafters and beams can be used as a ceiling in many different designs; how they are patterned should be considered if the rafters and beams will be left exposed.

Exposed-beam ceilings are usually made with 4 × 6 or 4 × 8 redwood or cedar timbers, although pine or oak can be used. If you are going to install a beamed ceiling, the design should emulate actual beam construction. Space the beams evenly or off-center, or for a unique look, place one beam across the center, and have the other beams butting into it from either side.

If there is an existing ceiling of plaster, adding beams can eliminate the plain look (beams do blend well with plaster), and if the beams are placed strategically, you may not have to repair the plaster cracks that you have been staring at for years. Beams can also be arranged on any finished ceiling, including a tiled ceiling.

OPENING A CEILING

For our project (see Drawing 9-1), we replaced my kitchen ceiling, which was a conventional, flat one. However, my house has a gambrel roof. We removed the ceiling (which was more mess than work) and found that the existing roof construction was satisfactory—there were collar beams and sufficient bracing. But because we were going to extend the ceiling height to 12 feet, we needed some additional planks to be sure the structural members would support the roof load. We installed 4 × 8 tie beams for both bracing and looks and stapled fiberglass batts (for insulation) against the existing 2 × 4 roof framing. Then we installed ½″ plasterboard over the fiberglass insulation, finishing with drywall tape and plaster.

BEAMED CEILING

You can easily install a beamed ceiling in one day. Use 2 × 4 beams for large rooms, thinner ones for smaller rooms. Steps 1 to 4 in Drawing 9-2 show how simple this construction is.

CEILING INSULATION

With today's heating and air-conditioning costs, you should insulate your ceilings. As shown in Drawing 9-3, insulation comes in many forms; the batten type is the easiest for the amateur to install. If the ceiling joists are exposed and accessible from the attic, all you have to do is lay in batts or other insulation. If you cannot get to the ceiling joists, nail insulation directly to the ceiling, as shown in step 2C of Drawing 9-3.

To insulate means to cover, line or separate with a material to prevent the passage, transfer or leakage of heat, cold, electricity or sound. The material used is called insulation. Today, because of increasing energy costs, more and more homeowners are retrofit insulating. But it does pay to learn about the different materials and then use what you consider the best one for your purposes; not only can insulating your home lower your energy bills, but your local power company may even pay part of the cost of insulation—check with your local energy office.

Fiberglass is sold in batts or blankets, each form having an aluminum backing or sometimes tar paper or cardboard. Blankets are difficult to install because their size is cumbersome. Batts are generally easier to install. With either blankets or batts, you must wear gloves and a safety mask; fiberglass particles can irritate and penetrate skin, and the particles will be in the air when you are working with the material.

Cellulose and perlite are sold as loose fill, in bags. They are easy to install: They are usually blown into the spaces that need insulation. Note that loose-fill cellulose can be dangerous because it becomes a fire hazard when it shrinks. Rock wool (mineral wool) is also installed by being blown in.

Polystyrene boards and urethane foam boards make excellent insulation. They come in widths of 16″, 18″ and 24″, in ½″ to 6″ in thicknesses. The disadvantages of these materials are that they are not fireproof and they require gypsum fireproof wallboards.

Installing Insulation

Any kind of insulation should be installed so it fills the voids between the rafters in the ceiling and the roof, in wall cavities, between floors, and so on. Unfilled gaps defeat the purpose of insulation. Batt or loose-fill insulation can easily be installed in walls of older homes without taking down the walls by blowing in the insulation between the 2 × 4s. In a new home, drywall or batts are stapled in place.

When using loose fill in an older home, remove the siding and drill 3- or 4-

OPENING UP A CEILING

Not all roofs are gambrelled, but all roofs work on the same geometric and structural principals. Whatever style of rafters you have, remember to pay attention to the horizontal ties and collars.

❶ Before removing or replacing any structural members, verify with local building department or with a qualified professional.

Special Note: Existing structure may be exposed as it is, or it may be simplified by using fewer and stronger structural members.

EACH SITUATION WILL REQUIRE A SPECIAL SOLUTION.

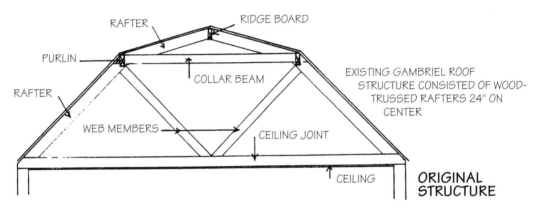

RAFTER — RIDGE BOARD
PURLIN
COLLAR BEAM
RAFTER
WEB MEMBERS →
CEILING JOINT
CEILING
EXISTING GAMBRIEL ROOF STRUCTURE CONSISTED OF WOOD-TRUSSED RAFTERS 24" ON CENTER
ORIGINAL STRUCTURE

❷ Remove ceiling. Remove and replace existing structural members.

❸ Insulate ceiling with 6" fiberglass batts stapled to rafters.

❹ Sheath ceiling with ½" gypsum board. Finish with drywall tape and plaster

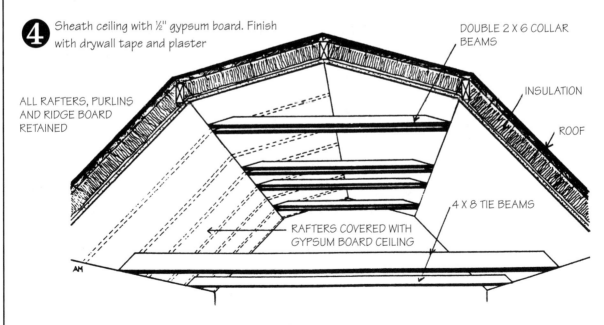

ALL RAFTERS, PURLINS AND RIDGE BOARD RETAINED

DOUBLE 2 X 6 COLLAR BEAMS

INSULATION

ROOF

4 X 8 TIE BEAMS

RAFTERS COVERED WITH GYPSUM BOARD CEILING

ADDING BEAMS TO A CEILING

Beams can be "built-up" out of several boards or they can be solid wood. Either way, make sure you have a helper and two stepladders on hand.

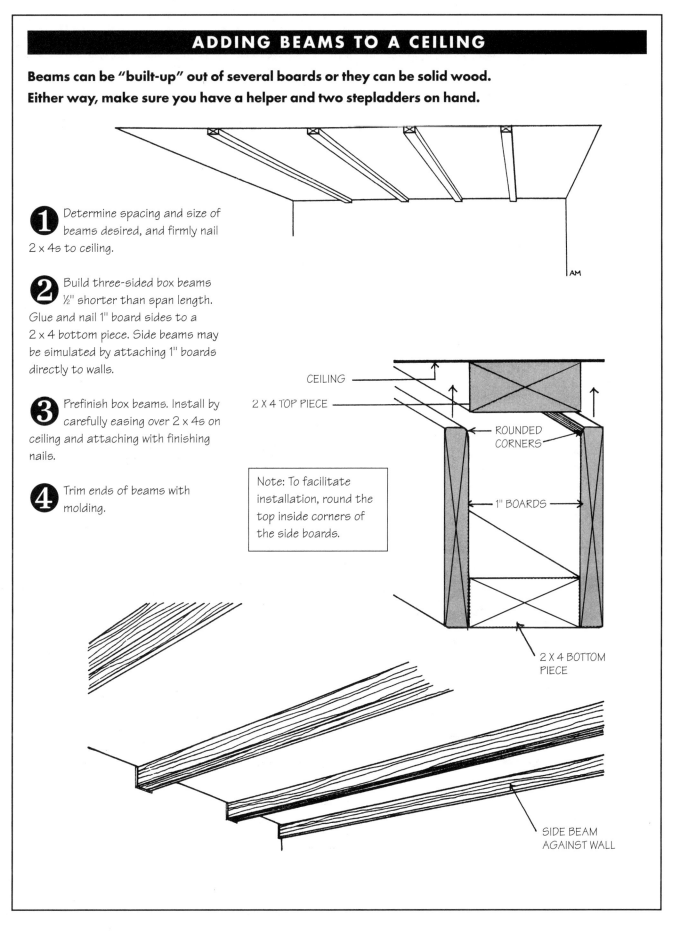

1 Determine spacing and size of beams desired, and firmly nail 2 x 4s to ceiling.

2 Build three-sided box beams ½" shorter than span length. Glue and nail 1" board sides to a 2 x 4 bottom piece. Side beams may be simulated by attaching 1" boards directly to walls.

3 Prefinish box beams. Install by carefully easing over 2 x 4s on ceiling and attaching with finishing nails.

4 Trim ends of beams with molding.

Note: To facilitate installation, round the top inside corners of the side boards.

CEILING

2 X 4 TOP PIECE

ROUNDED CORNERS

1" BOARDS

2 X 4 BOTTOM PIECE

SIDE BEAM AGAINST WALL

INSULATING CEILINGS

Whenever you open up an uninsulated wall, attic or ceiling — insulate. The cost is a minimal addition to the total project.

 Types of Insulation.

A. **Batt or Blanket:** Wood fibers, glass or mineral wood (fiberglass) may be faced or enclosed by paper or aluminum and is available with a vapor barrier. Usual sizes: 3 ½" (walls) or 6" thick (ceilings), 15" or 23" wide and 4' (batts) to 50' long (blankets).

B. **Board or Sheet:** Wood, glass or mineral fibers (fiberboard), cork and foamed plastics (styrofoam). Available with vapor barriers. Usual sizes: ½" to 2" thick and 12" square to 4' x 8'.

C. **Loose Fill:** Vermiculite, perlite, glass or mineral wool, shredded wood (not recommended) and polystyrene beads. Polyethylene sheeting can be used as a vapor barrier.

 Insulating Ceilings.

A. If the ceiling joists are exposed and accessible from the attic, lay in batts or blankets, or pour in and rake loose fill or have it blown (professionally) into place.

BATTS OR BLANKETS

LOOSE FILL

POLYETHYLENE VAPOR BARRIER

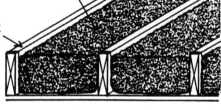

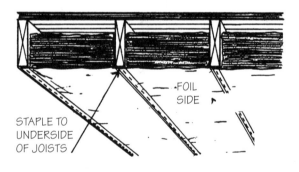

FOIL SIDE

STAPLE TO UNDERSIDE OF JOISTS

B. If the ceiling joists are accessible from below (before the ceiling is installed), staple faced batts or blankets.

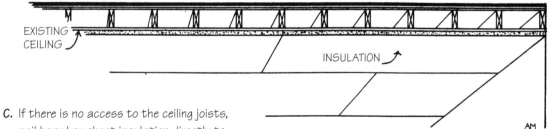

EXISTING CEILING

INSULATION

C. If there is no access to the ceiling joists, nail board or sheet insulation directly to the ceiling.

inch holes between studs or into existing wall frames. Empty the bags of material into a rented pumping machine and pump the fill into the holes. Close each hole with a plug and replace the siding. *Be sure to wear a safety mask to prevent inhaling the loose fill.* Or hire out the job.

Base your selection of insulation on the *R* factor (insulation) of the material. This number indicates how well the material will insulate. For maximum insulation, select a material with an R30 factor. Remember, the higher the factor, the more money you will save. The *R* value you select will depend on where you live and the type of heat you use, as well as the type of construction. For example, electric radiant heat dictates a higher *R* factor than oil hot-water heat.

Any insulation you select should have a vapor barrier of plastic or foil. The vapor barrier side of the insulation should always face the heated areas (inside) of the home. If using batts, buy those that are foil backed because the foil reflects heat.

CHAPTER TEN

FLOORS

Floors are the picture canvases of the home, the areas immediately viewed upon entrance. Floors can add to or detract from the total impression, depending on whether they are barren expanses of concrete (hardly aesthetic), carpeting, or wood in various patterns. The crafted look is most apparent in a handsome wood parquet or plank floor, which adds dimension and design to any home. Carpet, too, has a decorative effect. The five projects in this chapter will get you started installing attractive wood floors, but first let us consider floors in detail.

CONSTRUCTION

The basic construction is the same for most styles of wood floors; only the type of wood and patterns differ. Wooden floors have joists, headers, bridging, a subfloor and the flooring material. The joists form the floor's skeleton and are 2×6s, 2×8s or 2×10s placed on edge, usually on 12- or 16-inch centers. The width depends on the span the joists must bridge. The ends of the joists are supported by either a basement wall or a foundation. If the span is too great for a single joist, a girder is put down the middle of the span; joists run from the walls on both sides to meet the girder, overlapping at the point where they meet. The girder is an 8×8, supported at the ends on the foundation; a column, maybe two, supports the girder at the middle.

The floor must take the weight of walls, so the joists must have some support.

CONSTRUCTION LANGUAGE

BLIND-NAILED: Nailing through wood so nailheads do not show.

BUILDING PAPER: Kraft paper used as insulation against moisture.

GROUT: Mortar used to fill joints between tile.

PARQUET: A patterned floor of an inlay of different geometrically shaped woods.

PLANED: Surfaced and smooth.

SLEEPER: A board fixed to a concrete floor to serve as support for flooring.

SUBFLOOR: Rough plywood; finished flooring is laid on top of this.

VAPOR BARRIER: Usually aluminum foil or kraft paper used to prevent water vapor from penetrating to walls or floor.

Wherever there is a joist under a wall, the joist is doubled by spiking together two members. Bridging is used between the joists to keep them stiff and upright. Bridging is usually a 1 × 3 nailed in a cross position to the top of one joist and to the bottom of the joist next to it. Bridging increases the rigidity of the floor by distributing stress up and down the joists laterally.

If joists rest on basement walls or a foundation, headers are used to hold the joists vertically. Headers are 2″ planks spiked across the ends of the joists. The header is fastened to a sill, which is a wooden member that runs along the top of a masonry wall.

SUBFLOORING

Years ago, the subfloor was the floor—the boards were merely nailed to joists. Today floors are plywood (not good for final surfacing) or individual boards. Board subflooring is ¾″ or 1″ thick by 4″, 6″ or 8″ wide, square edged or regular tongue-and-groove. Subflooring boards are often applied either diagonally or perpendicular to joists. Just how you put in your subfloor will determine the direction the wood-finish flooring takes. On a diagonally laid subflooring, the flooring can be applied horizontally or perpendicular to joists, but on a perpendicular subflooring, the flooring has to be laid at right angles. Be sure subflooring boards end over the joists' end, and use tongue-and-groove boards or plywood. Plywood subflooring comes in several sizes; the size used is dictated by the joist spacing and the type and direction of finish flooring.

LAYING THE FLOORING

Once the subfloor is in, you can lay asphalt-impregnated paper (building paper—it lessens noise and cold) across the direction the strips will go down. Use a 3-inch overlap for the paper at the seams.

Although there are many materials for floors, wood is still considered the best possible floor for appearance and durability. Oak is generally the wood used for flooring and comes in strips 2¼″ wide by $^{25}/_{32}$″ thick (widths vary somewhat). Planks are also used in flooring. (These are discussed later.)

The oak strips are tongue-and-groove and end matched (this means the ends as well as the long edges are tongued and grooved). Oak flooring is available in several grades from clear to common, which has blemishes and some knots. You will also find strip flooring available in hard pine and fir, but oak will give you a better look.

1. Install strip flooring at right angles to the floor joists. Lay the first strip ½ inch from the edge of the wall; this space allows for expansion and contraction.

2 Face nail the first strip; use flooring nails that are long enough to go through the subfloor and into the joist by at least an inch. The first strip is nailed through the groove at an angle.

3. When the first strip is down, the grooved side of the second strip is forced into the tongue, and the tongue of the second strip is nailed in place. Since strips come in various lengths, each strip must be completed in one phase, or from wall to wall.

4. Many times the last strip that goes down must be cut lengthwise (ripped) to fit properly. Again be sure the edge is ½ inch from the wall for expansion purposes. Most oak flooring comes unfinished, and sanding is necessary to make each strip level with the next strip and to ensure a smooth floor.

It is vital that the first strip or board be absolutely straight and parallel to the wall or the line based at the room center. Remember that the entire floor is based on that first row. Always let the tongue of the board lead toward the center of the room.

If you are using 3″ or 4″ boards and want to start at the center line, you can still start at one edge. Here, the first strip of flooring must be ripped to the proper width to accommodate the widths of the room and the material.

As mentioned, use special flooring nails for floors; they are harder and slimmer than regular nails and spiral or ringed for extra holding power. Remember that the nails go into the *V* where the tongue meets the edge of the strip. Nail at a 45° angle.

Always bear in mind that wood expands and contracts with the amount of moisture in the air. Bring in wood strips that are to be installed at least a few weeks before you start work so they will have time to expand or contract in accordance with the humidity in the room.

Sanding floors is not easy. You must work with large, cumbersome machines that you are not familiar with. If you decide to sand your own floor, go easy, be patient and remember: *Never* sand across the grain. This goes for any type of sanding. One good stroke across the grain can mean hours of sanding with the grain to repair the damage. I won't sand my own floors. Experienced tradespeople can do a better job, can do it in one third the time, and bring their own tools so I don't need to rent anything or go anywhere.

Wood Plank Floor

This distinctive floor is appropriate for almost any room. Plank flooring is available in various kinds of woods and in different sizes, and it is prefinished, so there are many ways to make a bare floor interesting. Planking is laid almost in the same manner as strip flooring, with a few minor exceptions.

As we show in Drawing 10-1, you can put the flooring directly on a plywood subfloor, or, if the floor is concrete, put sleepers (2 × 4s) on the concrete over a vapor barrier (available at suppliers). Start with the groove side ¼ inch from the wall to allow for expansion; surface nail at the wall, and nail at the tongue. Nail the ends, and screw and plug them with matching or contrasting hardwood plugs. Stagger joints to create a hand-hewn effect. Blind nail the boards—the last boards should have the tongue planed off and be top nailed at the wall edge.

If the flooring is prefinished, no sanding or stain is required. To my eye, the natural look is best, so use a clear finish such as varathene. (Ask your hardware dealer.) Install baseboards.

PARQUET FLOOR

If you want a unique look, consider a parquet floor. Parquet squares now come in prefinished or tongue-and-groove styles; the 12″ × 12″ is perhaps the most popular size. Be sure the floor you are going to cover is absolutely level and clean. If it is not level, cover the floor with ⅜″ plywood with staggered joints to keep it level. (This may seem an unnecessary expense if there is an existing floor, but it saves headaches later.) Starting along the longest wall, mark a chalk line 12½ inches from the wall (the ½ inch is for expansion). (See Drawing 10-2.) Mark a second line at 90°. Apply the adhesive recommended, being careful not to cover chalk lines. Start at one end, ½ inch from the corner, and continue across with squares. Spread the adhesive evenly and smoothly, neither too thick nor too thin. Do one row at a time, and trim the last piece to fit. Clean away any excess adhesive with the solvent suggested by the manufacturer of the adhesive or the retailer from whom you purchased the material.

TILE FLOOR

You will find three types of ceramic tile available for flooring: glazed (smooth), mosaic and quarry; pick the one that suits your taste and budget. Follow the eight steps in Drawing 10-3. If the floor is wood, be sure to install two layers of sheathing with a primer. If the floor is concrete, be sure it is smooth and clean. Measure to find the midpoint of each wall; mark the midpoints of length and width with chalk lines. Now lay a row of loose tiles along each chalk line, and use a spacer or template to determine the joint (widths between tiles). Adjust the rows so the end tiles will be the same width; re-mark, if necessary, the other

WOOD PLANK FLOOR

Bring your knee-pads or an old couch cushion. Flooring workers, like sports professionals, have short careers. Special flooring nailers are available by tool renters in hammer-driven, electric or air-powered models.

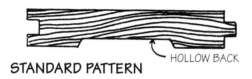

STANDARD PATTERN — HOLLOW BACK

Note: Plank flooring is available in various woods and sizes, as well as prefinished. (Strip flooring is similar, but narrower than 3½".)

1 Flooring can be laid directly on a plywood or board subfloor (a layer of building paper to make the floor draft-free is optional). If the floor is concrete, sleepers must be attached and a vapor barrier should be used.

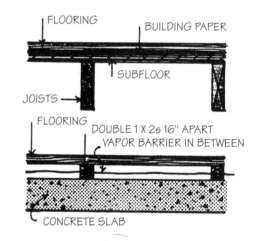

FLOORING — BUILDING PAPER — SUBFLOOR — JOISTS

FLOORING — DOUBLE 1 X 2s 16" APART VAPOR BARRIER IN BETWEEN — CONCRETE SLAB

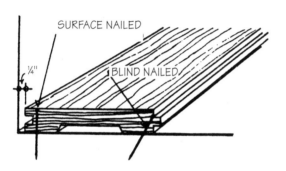

SURFACE NAILED — BLIND NAILED — ¼"

2 Starting with groove side ¼" from the wall to allow for expansion, carefully surface nail at the wall and blind nail at the tongue.

3 Ends should be blind nailed and/or screwed and plugged with matching or contrasting hardwood plugs. Joints should be staggered.

PLUGS OVER SCREWS — JOINT — SUBFLOOR

4 Continue blind nailing boards and use matching thresholds at the doorways. Last boards should have the tongue planed off and be top nailed at the wall edge

5 If the flooring is not prefinished, sand if required, stain or leave it natural, and use a clear finish made especially for floors (follow the manufacturer's directions).

6 Install baseboard ¾" wide at the bottom to hide the surface-nailed perimeter. Finish to match the floor.

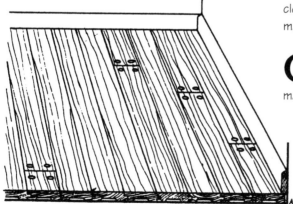

INSTALLING A PARQUET FLOOR

**The most important thing here is to lay out the chalk lines as perfectly as possible.
Use your square and don't hesitate to erase and restrike a line.**

Note: Parquet comes in various prefinished tongue-and-groove hardwood tile sizes.

CHALK LINES

90°

1 Floor to be covered must be smooth, level and clean. Otherwise sheath with ⅜" plywood or particle board with joints staggered.

2 Start along the longest wall and mark a chalk line 12½" from the wall. Allow a ½" space at perimeter for expansion (baseboard will hide gap). Mark a second line at 90°.

3 Apply special adhesive, being careful not to cover chalk lines. Follow manufacturer's directions.

NOTCHED TROWEL →

ADHESIVE SHOULD BE SPREAD EVENLY AND NOT TOO THICKLY.

4 Start at one end ½" from corner. Continue across, and trim last piece to fit. Repeat, one row at a time, being careful not to walk on or shift tiles. Clean any excess adhesive.

5 Use matching hardwood thresholds at doorways.

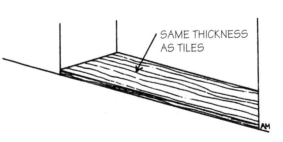

SAME THICKNESS AS TILES

6 If last few rows are not easily accessible, lay a sheet of plywood on top of the tiles to distribute your weight, and carefully finish the floor, cutting the last row to fit with a ½" space at the wall.

7 Wait until the floor is set before walking on it. Then install the baseboard (¾" wide at the bottom).

chalk line so it falls along a joint. Repeat the same procedure in the opposite direction.

Starting from the center, and without covering any chalk lines, spread tile adhesive smoothly and evenly with a trowel. Working in one section at a time, lay the tiles, using the spacers to space joints. After the tiles are dry and set, fill in the joints with grout (powdered or premixed). The grouting takes patience and time, and it is not as easy to put down as it may seem—be careful. After the grout has set, clean the floor thoroughly and apply a sealer.

REFINISHING A WOOD FLOOR

If you already have a wood floor you like but which needs some help, refinish it. If you have decided to do it yourself, then I'll tell you how. Remove existing old finish with stripper, and rent an electric drum sander (see Drawing 10-4).

1. Use a coarse 20-grit paper, and sand with the grain. Maneuver the sander slowly and with equal pressure; it takes strong wrists or the sander will work away from you, leaving small valleys that will show and detract from the floor's beauty.
2. Use a sanding block for sanding corners and along walls.
3. When the first sanding is finished, clean the floor of dust and repeat the procedure, sanding with 40-grit paper.
4. For the final sanding (after cleaning the floor again), use 100-grit sandpaper.
5. Now thoroughly clean the floor of dust and apply a *stain* with a brush, or use a *clear finish*. (See Drawing 10-4 for full details.)

You can choose among several clear finishes for floor treatment at suppliers. These protective coatings, which go under various trade names, are easy to apply and, more importantly perhaps, easy to maintain. They wear well and offer a fine way to show off wood while protecting the surface.

ELEVATING A FLOOR AREA

Elevating a portion of an existing floor can beautify a room by breaking up the space and making small spaces seem larger. Once you decide what part of the floor you want to elevate:

1. Nail 2 × 4s, as shown in step 2 of Drawing 10-5, and side ledgers.

CERAMIC TILE FLOOR

If you are using thick quarry tile, you may need to rent a power tile saw. Complete the full-tile job first, then cut and install the perimeter pieces.

1 Floor structure should be sound, and if wood, it should have two layers of sheathing, with a primer applied to its surface. If concrete, floor should be smooth and clean.

2 Measure to find the midpoint of each wall, and with a chalk line, find and mark the center.

3 Lay a row of loose tiles along a chalk line. Use a template to determine the joint width (a board of the right thickness). Adjust row so that the end tiles will be the same width, and remark, if necessary, the other chalk line so it falls along a joint.

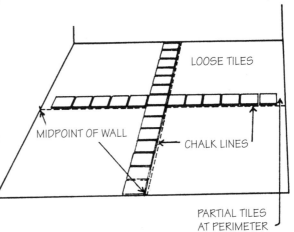

LOOSE TILES

MIDPOINT OF WALL

CHALK LINES

PARTIAL TILES
AT PERIMETER

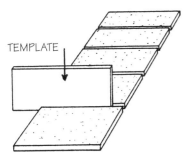

TEMPLATE

4 Repeat the same procedure in the opposite direction.

5 Cut any tiles required for the perimeter with a tile cutter. Any irregular cuts can be made with tile nippers.

6 Starting from the center and without covering the chalk lines, spread the tile adhesive with a notched trowel to achieve the proper thickness as recommended by the manufacturer. Work in one quadrant at a time and lay the tiles, using the template to space the joints. Lay a sheet of plywood to walk over the tiles.

Note: Glazed, mosaic or quarry tiles or pavers may be used.

7 After the tiles are set, fill the joints with grout (powdered or premixed). Follow the manufacturer's directions. Smooth with a jointer, and clean any excess.

8 After the grout has set, clean the floor thoroughly. Apply a sealer if necessary, and install the baseboard.

DOUBLE FLOOR SHEATHING

ADHESIVE   TILE   GROUT

AM

FLATTENED END

JOINTER

REFINISHING A WOOD FLOOR

Power sanders are heavy and cumbersome machines. If you have a sheet of plywood around, practice on it before you start on your flooring.

1 Clear the room, tape any ducts and remove the baseboard. Check the floor boards so that they're tight, and countersink any exposed nails. Fill holes and cracks with wood putty.

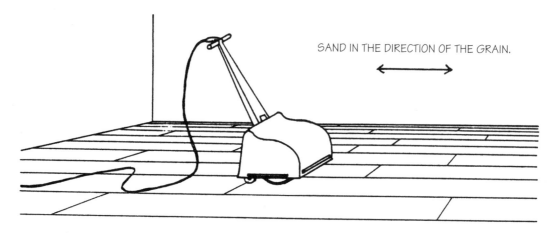

SAND IN THE DIRECTION OF THE GRAIN.

2 Use an electric drum sander with a coarse 20-grit sandpaper. Proceed slowly, and sand with the grain. Use a sanding block, a belt sander or a disc sander against the walls.

SANDPAPER TACKED TO BLOCK

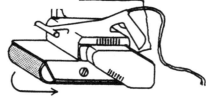

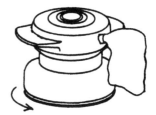

3 When the first sanding is finished, clean the floor of dust and repeat the same procedure, sanding with a medium, 40-grit sandpaper.

4 For the final sanding use a fine, 100-grit sandpaper.

5 Thoroughly clean the floor of dust. Leave natural or apply a stain with a brush (follow directions on the can).

BRUSH WITH THE GRAIN.

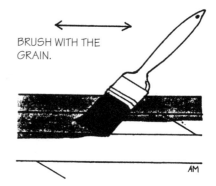

6 Apply a clear finish made especially for floors (follow the manufacturer's directions). Refinish the baseboard to match, and reinstall when the floor is thoroughly dry. As a final finish, use a slip-resistant paste wax and buff.

AM

2. Toenail double 2 × 4s. Make sure all tops of ledgers and girders are level. Use a carpenter's level.
3. As in step 3 of Drawing 10-5, set joists across the girders and ledgers at 16-inch centers. Start from the wall, and toenail the joists and ledgers in place.
4. Cover the raised platform with ½", 4 × 8 plywood; cover the plywood with carpeting or any other suitable material.

WOODEN SQUARES

If you do not want to pay for wooden boards or attempt the installation of a wood floor, try the 12″ × 12″ tongue-and-groove squares (plain-edge squares do not work well). With squares, you can get an interesting checkerboard effect. The woods available run the gamut from exotic cabinet woods to oak and plywood. Installation is a breeze: Today, many of the squares are self-adhesive, or you can buy adhesive.

ELEVATING A FLOOR AREA

Block underneath your joists as often as it feels necessary. Toenailed scraps will work fine for stiffening any spongy areas. Many times this type of floor is installed over an old garage floor, which may be very irregular.

Note: Check building codes for minimum ceiling height of raised area (usually 7'-6").

1 Determine area to be elevated and location of steps (necessary if height is more than 8").

2 Nail 2 x 4 plates at exposed perimeter. Nail side ledgers 4" below finished floor level, and toenail double 2 x 4 girders on 4 x 4 posts, 48" apart maximum. Tops of ledgers and girders should be level.

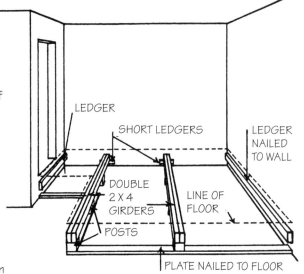

3 Set joists across the girders and ledgers at 16" on center, starting from the wall. Toenail in place (48" maximum span for 2 x 4 joists).

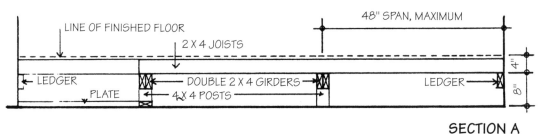

SECTION A

4 Sheath the exposed sides and top with ½" plywood. Stagger joints on top.

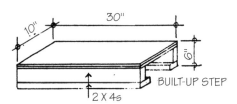

BUILT-UP STEP

5 Build a step so that each riser will be equal. Use 2 x 4s and plywood. Nail into place.

6 Carpet or otherwise finish platform and step.

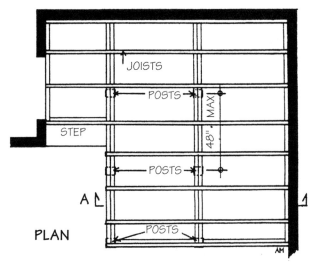

PLAN

CHAPTER ELEVEN

SUN-ROOMS

Whether you call it a *sun-room* and build it from scratch, or convert a porch and call it a *sun porch*, or design a solarium, this additional space will make your dwelling handsome, and it is a fine retreat from the busy world.

The sun-room is not new; it was a staple part of the old English house (sometimes also called a *conservatory*). It breaks the monotony of the typical house plan and creates comfortable, additional living space.

In this chapter, we discuss building a sun-room, whether glass enclosed or screened, to add to your existing dwelling, and also converting a porch into a sun-room.

LOCATION AND SIZE

The idea of the sun-room is to have a place that is situated to benefit from the rays of the sun—a comfort on chilly autumn mornings and cold winter afternoons. A southern exposure is what you want, but if this isn't possible, then a western exposure is a second choice, and an eastern, a third. Let's hypothesize that you do have space on the south side of the house.

Now that the location is determined, what about size? The average sun-room need not be large (indeed, it shouldn't be, because generally it will then be out of proportion to the rest

CONSTRUCTION LANGUAGE

ANCHOR BOLT: A metal spike projecting above concrete.

CONCRETE SLAB: Poured concrete used as floor.

CURED: Concrete that has dried for several days.

GYPSUM BOARD: A type of plasterboard.

HEADER: A beam or a board used to form an opening for a door, a window, etc.

LEDGER: A board that supports another piece of lumber.

MUDSILL: The bottom plate of a wall.

SHEATHING: The exterior surface of a wall.

TIE STRAPS: Metal strips to join two boards.

TONGUE-AND-GROOVE: A board with tongue in one edge and groove in the other.

TOP PLATE: A horizontal board doubled above a door and a window.

RABBET: A groove sawn or planed along the corner edge of a board.

of the house). A good size (and my sun-room is used as an example) is $10' \times 12'$ or $10' \times 14'$. This gives ample space for furniture and seating—and a few plants.

The room can adjoin almost any other room of the house; I have seen lovely sun-rooms next to the kitchen, the living room, and even a bedroom. In any case, it increases the actual footage of the house and further creates an illusion of space.

As a lean-to, it also eliminates building a fourth wall and requires only a three-wall construction.

Be careful when designing the enclosed space; do not make the room all glass. It will be too hot in summer and too cold in winter. A good idea is to make the south wall 30 percent glass; if you like (but it is not necessary), include top light by using skylights.

In essence, plan a bit by drawing sketches on paper before you decide on a specific place for the sun-room. Draw a basic floor plan of the house, and add the sun-room in several places until you come up with a definite location. Even the roughest sketch will give you some idea of proportion and scale.

Basic Construction

The basic construction of the sun-room requires footings and foundations. This may sound formidable, but it is not. The footing is simply a concrete wall or a slab to support the room. The formidable part of the footing is digging out the soil to prepare a level terrain for the pouring of the concrete. You can have the slab or footing poured professionally or tackle it yourself. I recommend that you have it poured professionally because it is a difficult job. It must be done quickly, and it requires more than one person to accomplish. Once the ground is prepared, forms for holding the concrete footing are put in place.

Footings

Footings and foundations anchor the building in the ground and act as a solid platform for the addition. (A *footing* is part of the foundation.) They are necessary for any type of room, and several types of footings are shown in Drawings 11-1 and 11-2. Footings for support vary and may be of slab construction, a footing-and-foundation wall, or a footing with a masonry wall. Whichever design you follow, excavation of existing soil will be necessary. So although designs may vary depending upon where you live and on local building codes, the following general plan can be used:

1. Drive twelve stakes 4 to 8 feet from the prospective dividing corners of the desired design. Then, using string, lay out the exact plan of the building from stake to stake.

2. Dig a trench around the desired perimeter of the proposed site. Make the trench approximately 2-feet wide and a minimum of 1-foot deep (or whatever building codes advise).

3. Once you have decided on the height of the foundation, use a level to be certain all stakes are equal. (*Note*: If possible, leave 3-inch holes in the base of the foundation about every 6 feet so water can run off to a lower grade. The drain should extend all around the exterior of the room at the base of the footing in the trench.)

4. Foundation-framing equipment is usually available on a rental basis. If not, use ¾″ plywood to frame the foundation. The width of the footing should be 8″ (or whatever local building codes require).

5. Reinforce floorings with steel rods laid horizontally and vertically within the footing. Pound the vertical rods into the ground between the foundation framing, and then, using wires, tie the horizontal rods to the vertical ones.

6. Leave ¼″ to ½″ "D" anchor bolts (available at lumberyards) protruding from the top of the footing so there will be a base to secure the bearing plate. The plate should be laid approximately 1 inch inside the outside line of the footing.

7. Apply a vapor seal to the top of the footing to stop capillary action.

8. Be sure there is an adequate drainage system at the base of and through the foundation or under the slab to carry off excess water.

9. For outside drainage, place drain tiles at the base and through the footings, on 4 to 6 inches of rough gravel.

10. For inside drainage, plan a floor drain (optional). Before the floor is installed, locate the drainage heads in a low area of the flooring.

Concrete Floors

Concrete is an economical and durable floor because it resists water spill if there are plants, and it retains heat. Always install a gravel or sand base; this provides a solid, level place for concrete to rest and helps eliminate cracks in the concrete. Over the gravel install a plastic sheet, which will act as a vapor barrier.

The floor is poured along with the foundation and should be at least 4 inches thick and reinforced with steel rods and wire mesh. Again, be sure the ground is absolutely level; otherwise, concrete can eventually develop cracks.

To build a concrete floor, you will need wooden forms forms to hold the

ADDING AN ENCLOSED SUN PORCH

Once your foundation and slab are in, the rest of the job can be done in weekends.

1 Determine the location and size of the room. Check the local building codes for the requirements concerning the concrete slab (size of footings, reinforcing, etc.) and the structure (types of materials, sizes of studs, posts, headers, beams, etc.).

2 Concrete slabs and footings should generally be done by professionals. This includes accurate layout, excavation, fill (if required), formwork, reinforcing, and the pouring and finishing of the concrete.

3 Once the concrete is cured, attach the 2 x 4 redwood or pressure-treated mudsill to the anchor bolts (except at doorways). The finished surface can be concrete or can be surfaced with ceramic tile.

Note: By using the area formed by two right-angle walls, only two additional walls need be built.

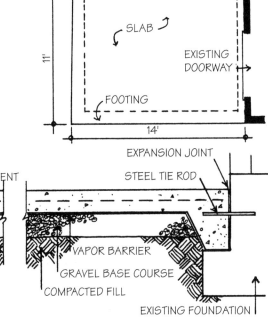

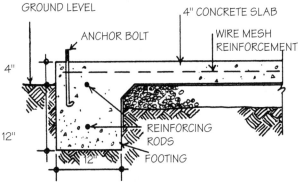

TYPICAL SLAB FLOOR

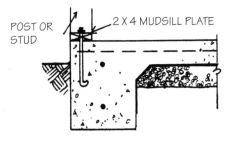

4 Frame in the new walls with 2 x 4 studs and 3 x 4 posts between the fixed glass windows. Set in a 4 x 6 header on studs over the french-door opening. Tie the whole with a double 2 x 4 top plate. The new structure should be tied into the existing structure with lag screws.

Buy your doors, windows, and brick or block flooring before you begin framing.

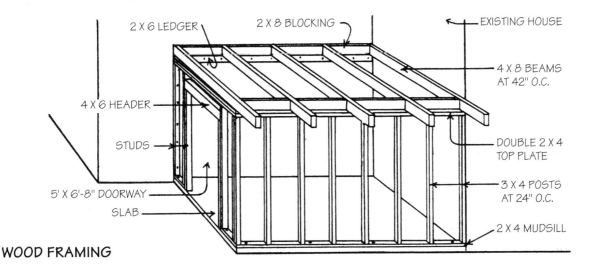

2 X 6 LEDGER

2 X 8 BLOCKING

EXISTING HOUSE

4 X 8 BEAMS AT 42" O.C.

4 X 6 HEADER

STUDS

DOUBLE 2 X 4 TOP PLATE

3 X 4 POSTS AT 24" O.C.

5' X 6'-8" DOORWAY

SLAB

2 X 4 MUDSILL

WOOD FRAMING

5 Attach a 2 x 6 ledger, with lag screws, to the existing house wall 2" higher than the opposite top plate so that the roof will have a slight slope. Set the 4 x 8 beams, with 2 x 8 blocking between, at the ledger and the top plate. Toenail in place.

6 Sheath the roof with 2 x 6 tongue-and-groove decking. Leave openings for skylights (see *Openings for a Skylight*). It is advisable to have the built-up roofing professionally installed. Be sure that there is flashing where the roof meets the house wall.

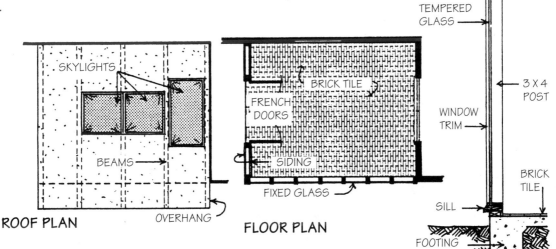

DECKING

BUILT-UP ROOF

BEAM

BLOCKING

TOP PLATE

TEMPERED GLASS

3 X 4 POST

WINDOW TRIM

BRICK TILE

SILL

FOOTING

SECTION

SKYLIGHTS

BEAMS

ROOF PLAN

OVERHANG

BRICK TILE

FRENCH DOORS

SIDING

FIXED GLASS

FLOOR PLAN

7 Use siding to match the house inside and out. Install the skylights (for good ventilation one should be operable), fixed windows, french doors and brick tiles. See *Prefabricated Skylight, Windows, French Doors and Ceramic Tile Floor*.

concrete until it sets. You can build your own forms, but in most parts of the country, you can rent them. The forms must be put in place absolutely level with the top wood board at floor level. Reinforcing steel rods must go around the footing; these support the weight of the building and anchor it.

You can mix your own concrete for a small area ($5' \times 10'$) by renting a power mixer and putting in cement, sand and gravel. The usual proportion is one part cement to two parts sand to two parts gravel or aggregate. Into the mixer put water, then gravel, then sand, finishing with the cement. The job must be done quickly, before drying sets in, and the floor must be smoothed at one time.

For larger areas, buy ready-mixed concrete and have it delivered to the site. A truck generally holds about 7 yards; the concrete runs from the chute directly into the site where you have the forms in place. (You can also have companies pump concrete up a hill or into inaccessible places, but that will, of course, cost more money.) Ready-mixed concrete is a boon, but you must be prepared to work fast, within a 30-minute period, or you will get charged overtime. Try to have three people on hand; one to guide the chute (or the truck driver might do this), and two with floats and trowels to get the mix in place. If concrete starts to set before you have finished the pour, you are in trouble, so keep working—and fast. As the pour is being done, take sticks and poke into the footings to be sure concrete gets to all voids in trenches.

Distributing the concrete at a uniform level in the form area is known as *screeding*. This is done with a *screed board* (two pieces of wood nailed to each other—a 2×4 with a 1×2 handle).

1. Use the screed board (and wear rubber boots) to level the concrete as it is poured.
2. Push and pull the board to achieve the level surface. Keep a flat-nosed shovel on hand in case the pouring gets ahead of you and too much concrete is dumped at one time.
3. Tamp down the concrete; run an expanded metal screen over the concrete to level the slab and bring water, sand and cement to the surface.
4. Use a *float* (a 2×6 wooden board with a handle) to further level the concrete. Work it over large areas while the concrete is still wet. Do not dig it in; use a light touch. Be sure the handle of the float is long enough to reach the middle of the area of the slab from the outer edge. Use the float again when the concrete is sugary or somewhat set, and work in wide sweeps to level the slab. Steel troweling is the final step; this seals and waterproofs the slab and gets rid of minor defects. When the concrete is set (time depends on climate and type of pour—generally 24 hours), remove the wooden forms. For a few days, especially if the weather is hot, cover the area with plastic.

CONVERTING A PORCH

An existing porch can easily become a sun-room, and actually little extra construction is needed. The basic foundation is already in place, so only walls and a roof are necessary.

1. Generally, the structural posts (usually 4 × 4s) are already in place; remove the railing if there is one.
2. Decide on the number of windows and their locations.
3. Frame the openings as explained in the window chapter.
4. Toenail 2 × 4 studs on each side of the window openings; put in a 2 × 4 soleplate at bottom and a 2 × 4 sill, with cripple studs in between them. (See Drawings 11-3 and 11-4.) Remember that solid walls need studs every 16 inches on center.

When the framing of the openings is completed, apply appropriate exterior material that matches or contrasts pleasantly with the rest of the house. Nail in place and finish accordingly. You may want to install flashing along the roof line. Finish the interior walls using proper insulation and fiberboard; tape and paint.

There may be an existing roof on the porch, which you can use as is. If you have to replace the roof, think about that skylight.

GLASS AND GLAZING

Because the sun-porch is built with some glass, it is wise to know something about the material. Thermopane glass is highly recommended, to conserve as much heat as possible in winter. This is two pieces of glass hermetically sealed, with an air space in between. These units come in clear glass in thicknesses of ⅛", ¼" and so on, or in patterned glass in different thicknesses. Thermopane is available in standard sizes ranging from 16" × 20" to very large dimensions; before you start to design or build, it is wise to have a list of the standard thermopane sizes. Custom units made to size are 25 to 40 percent higher and take much more time to get than standard stock sizes.

Glass is available as ⅛" or 3/16" crystal quality. This is a rolled glass, which means it will have some waves, but this is not objectionable in small sizes. In large sizes, it is better to use ¼" polished plate glass. This glass is polished on both sides in order to prevent waviness and presents a clear image when you look through it.

CONVERTING A PORCH INTO A SUN-ROOM

An old porch is a great place to use salvaged double-hung windows. Even if your old porch is nothing more than a patio slab, the first task — the floor — has already been done.

Note: Before enclosing any existing porch, consult your local building department.

Old windows can be used to enclose the porch. As many as possible should be operable for good ventilation.

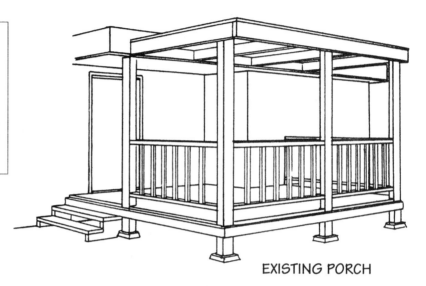

EXISTING PORCH

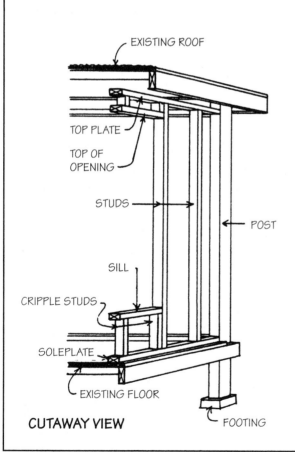

EXISTING ROOF

TOP PLATE

TOP OF OPENING

STUDS

POST

SILL

CRIPPLE STUDS

SOLEPLATE

EXISTING FLOOR

FOOTING

CUTAWAY VIEW

1 Remove the existing railings, but do not remove any structural posts. If any diagonal braces at the top of the posts are to be removed, they should be replaced with steel tie straps.

2 Depending on the size of the windows and doors and their proposed locations, frame in the openings, starting with a 2 x 4 soleplate and a 2 x 4 top plate nailed into place.

3 Toenail 2 x 4, full-height studs on either side of each opening. Then nail a 2 x 4 across the top of each opening and at the windowsill level.

4 Solid wall areas should have studs no more than 16" on center. Also, there should be cripple studs above and below the openings.

5 When the framing is finished, sheath the exterior solid walls to match the existing house siding. Be sure to install flashing where required. Insulate the wall from the interior with fiberglass batts.

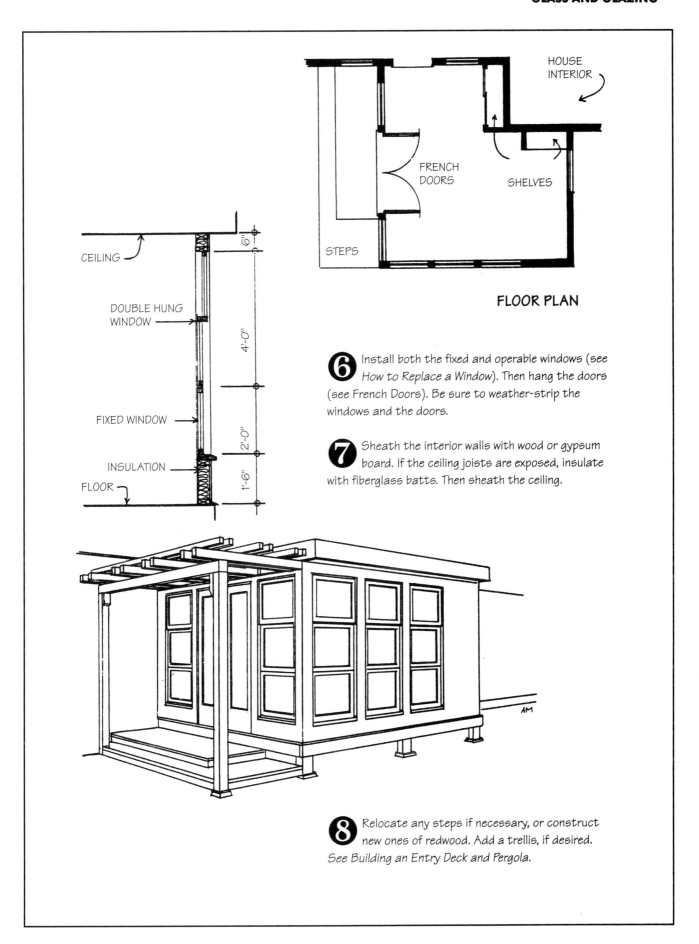

HOUSE
INTERIOR

FRENCH
DOORS

SHELVES

STEPS

FLOOR PLAN

CEILING

DOUBLE HUNG
WINDOW

FIXED WINDOW

INSULATION

FLOOR

6"

4'-0"

2'-0"

1'-6"

6 Install both the fixed and operable windows (see *How to Replace a Window*). Then hang the doors (see French Doors). Be sure to weather-strip the windows and the doors.

7 Sheath the interior walls with wood or gypsum board. If the ceiling joists are exposed, insulate with fiberglass batts. Then sheath the ceiling.

8 Relocate any steps if necessary, or construct new ones of redwood. Add a trellis, if desired. *See Building an Entry Deck and Pergola.*

When using wood frames for glass (as most often is the case), be sure the wooden members are rabbeted to accommodate the thickness of the glass. This should be one-piece construction and not two separate pieces of wood. Glass is set into the rabbet (generally ¼-inch deep), and then putty is installed. This type of glazing assures a seal-tight window. For a more thorough discussion of glass, see page 61.

ROOFING

The roof is one of the more important parts of a sun-room. Its design may be gabled, A-frame, vaulted, sawtooth or simply at a 45° angle (against a house wall). The roof should contain at least 30 percent glass to admit sufficient light and this may be in the form of skylights, or clerestory (upper) windows, or simply domes.

Clerestory windows are a good idea because they are set like ordinary windows and should not leak. Flat glass set in wooden panels is yet another way to approach roof design, but these, like peaked or canted skylights, are difficult to build and, further, generally leak water. Plastic domes of many different shapes are available, too, and they seem to be airtight and leakproof.

No matter what you decide to use, wood or metal framing to accommodate the glass or domes is necessary; this in turn must be adequately protected with metal flashing to eliminate the possibility of water seeping into the structure.

In any area where glass is in the ceiling, building codes require the use of tempered or wire glass. This is much more costly than standard window glass. In clerestory windows, double-strength or thermopane window glass is generally allowed, but to be sure, check with local building offices.

Glass must be put in place properly; this is done with putty or equivalent glazing compounds and glazing clips. The glass sits on the putty and is the cushion for it. To further assure an airtight enclosure, plastic cushioning tape is frequently used.

If replacing old glass:

1. Remove old putty or glazing compound.
2. Scrape and chisel the recess (rabbet) where the glass goes.
3. Lay a thin bead of putty or compound in the rabbet.
4. Install the measured pane of glass firmly against the compound.
5. Secure it in place with glazing clips in place every 8 inches or so.
6. Place a thin bead of compound against the glass and smooth it out; press with a putty knife against the rabbet.

CHAPTER TWELVE

OUTDOOR ADDITIONS

DECKS

Decks are part of garden construction, and they are worthwhile additions to any property, especially on hillsides. But whether at a low level or on the side of a steep hill, a deck brings nature into the home.

A deck must be built solidly and with careful consideration of weight factors. An ill-conceived deck will be shaky and undesirable as an addition to the home. A deck must also have guard rails with a minimum height of 30 inches and be capable of resisting a load of 20 pounds per lineal foot acting at the top. General building codes for decks specify that "the floor must be designed to support 40 pounds per square foot of surface in addition to the weight of the deck."

Building codes for decks vary by city; check your local building office for specific information. The planning and construction data offered here are general and not to be construed as legal limitations.

The four kinds of decks are:

1. platform in the yard
2. a hillside deck (attached to the house)
3. a rooftop deck
4. a ground-level deck (patio)

The construction is somewhat different for each type of deck. Concrete decks are often built, but we'll discuss wooden decks, which are more popular.

LOCATION

Scout the site to determine the best place for a deck; this will vary depending on the situation. To best determine the location of the future deck, observe the sun as it strikes your property. Once you have an idea of sunny and shady areas, orient your deck accordingly. You can put a deck in any exposure and then combat the weather with overhangs and other roof protection. Remember, though, that a deck should be a deck, not a built-up outside shelter.

It is often difficult to decide how large the deck should be, but an easy rule to follow is to make the deck three-fourths as large as the room it adjoins — it will always be in scale with the rest of the house. A 16′ × 20′ living room accommodates a 12′ × 16′ deck very well and looks handsome.

CONSTRUCTION

Typical construction of a low-level deck is usually posts on footings or piers. The footings anchor the deck to the site and keep lumber away from contact with the soil. Footings must extend below the frost line because water in the concrete will crack the footings when they freeze. Depending upon your location, for a small ground-level deck you can use precast footings or concrete blocks bought at suppliers. (Casting your own footings is difficult.)

For the hillside deck, footings must extend at least 30 inches below grade and be 1 foot or more across. These footings should contain steel reinforcing bars to hold the weight of the deck.

Footings for decks must be placed absolutely level in position so the structure will have no tilt. Ideally, the deck should be almost level with the house floor.

To build a deck, measure and then outline the area with string and stakes.

1. Determine your first corner-post location and put a stake in place; run a line of nylon string to the next posthole location.
2. Put in a stake at this second corner; continue until all corners have stakes.
3. Now, with a posthole digger or a shovel, dig down at least 20 inches (check with local building offices to determine frost line). Dig to the appropriate depth and set the footings in place.

The 4 × 4 post is the one most used for ground-level decks; it bears a load weight of 8,000 pounds up to a height of 8 feet. Hillside decks bear heavier, loads, so substantially heavier posts — 6 × 6s or even 8 × 8s — are necessary. Local building departments can advise you as to which size posts to use, or you can get this information from your lumberyard.

Post heights must be accurate. The substructure must be level, even and stable to support the horizontal deck platform with ease. On the house wall, mark a line that will be flush with the top of the deck surface. Measure down the thickness of the decking you are going to use; then add the thickness of the joists to find the top of the ledger height.

To set posts in place, align them so they are absolutely straight; use a carpenter's level. Now run a line from the ledger to the post and mark it. From that mark, subtract the depth of the support beam and make a new mark. Now take down the post and cut off the excess.

Cross bracing is needed to prevent the deck from moving vertically. Use heavy-duty post connectors between each post and beam to supply the necessary support.

Beams can be toenailed to posts or fastened with strap metal or joist hangers, which come in L-shaped, T-shaped or straight pieces. Joists that will run lengthwise can be placed on top of the beams or attached flush with their tops.

THE DECK-BUILDING PROCESS

Standard deck construction is an 11-step procedure:

1. Establish the location of the foot as we described.
2. Dig holes to the proper depth; locate the marker lines.
3. Place the pier forms in position, and level them with each other, using a level line.
4. Establish the desired level of the deck, and measure down the depth of the decking plus the joists. Mark the ledger and secure it to the stud, starting at the center.
5. After determining the heights, set the posts and check for plumb, using a carpenter's level on two sides.
6. With a piece of scrap lumber set on the posts, check to be sure all the parts in the row are on an even plane.
7. With a measuring tape or string, check the level between the ledger and the beam to see that they are flush.
8. Secure the post to the connector.
9. Place the beam on the post, and toenail it in place.
10. Use the house wall as the base point to ensure that decking will be true. Be sure first that the board is a straight line.
11. Nail the boards in place, using a spacer (a block of wood) between each board to ensure even spaces.

Decking is $\frac{5}{4} \times 4$, $\frac{5}{4} \times 6$, 2×4 or 2×6 stock, and it is set with uniform space between each board nailed on joists; the joists in turn are nailed to beams, and the beams are attached to posts on piers. These essential steps of deck building can be adapted to other typical deck designs.

PATIO

A patio is an extension of the home and a delightful place to spend time away from a busy world. Patios are rarely expensive if you do most of the work yourself, and you do not have to be very handy with tools to install a modest patio.

Basically the patio is a courtyard without a fence and open to the sky; it is common in Spanish architecture, generally in the center of the house. The Americanized version has put the patio as an adjunct to the house, which may be on any exposure—a simple exposed area with a few plants (sometimes furniture) adjacent to the living room or dining area, or a partially enclosed area.

The patio generally has a brick or tile floor, slate or concrete, perhaps an overhead to create a decorative statement, and some appropriate outdoor garden furniture to complete the picture. Container plants are usually placed on the patio to furnish needed green accent. The total effect is of a room that is attractive and part of the home, adding square footage to the living plan.

Size and Location

To decide where the patio will be, consider the effects of the sun, wind and rain. A west patio, for example, that received the sun almost every day would be too warm for your personal use by day. A patio on the northwest side of the house may be too windy, and a south patio basks in the sun—in chilly climates, this can be a blessing, but in hot climates it becomes an annoyance. A patio that faces east is the ideal location; there is morning sun, but in the afternoon it is cool and shady.

A patio puts the finishing touch to a home, but don't make it so large it becomes a bleak expanse of gray concrete. And don't make it too small; it will then appear like a tacked-on, postage-stamp area. For the standard 2000 square-foot house, a patio of 15' × 20' is fine. This is large enough to accommodate various activities and not so small it would feel crowded.

PATIO PAVINGS

There are several patio pavings—tile brick, concrete, flagstone, slate. What you select depends on your pocketbook and the overall setting you are trying to achieve. Avoid loose fill materials, such as crushed rock or gravel, fir bark and such, which are temporary and have to be replaced periodically. Further, these materials are rarely attractive as patio floors.

Choose a patio floor that is in character with the house and is durable. You can install most patio floors yourself, although, if you choose concrete, I suggest you have it done professionally. It is generally not expensive and is a tough job for the do-it-yourselfer.

Here are some kinds of patio floors and their advantages and disadvantages.

Brick

This is a popular paving because it is handsome, easy to install, and lasts a long time. You can set brick in mortar or use the easy brick-on-sand installation. Brick comes in a variety of colors, in rough or smooth surfaces, glazed or unglazed. Choose a hard-burned rather than a green brick for outdoors. It should be dark red in color rather than salmon color, which indicates an underburned process and is less durable. Brick can be laid in different patterns — herringbone, basket weave, running bond — but don't get too fancy.

To install brick on sand:

1. Grade the soil with a board and tamp it down smoothly. Get rid of lumpy clay and debris.
2. Slope the floor away from the house — 1 inch to 6 feet of paving — to allow for drainage.
3. Put in a 2- to 3-inch bed of sand and level it.
4. Set the bricks as close together as possible, and check each row with a level as you go.
5. Dust sand into the cracks.

Brick can also be set in mortar, but this is usually a job for professionals.

The disadvantage of brick is that it becomes slippery in wet weather and can sometimes be expensive — anywhere from 16 cents a brick up!

Tile

Tile is smoother than brick and easier to clean; it has a lovely finished look that blends well with interior floorings, whether they be wood or tile. If the patio floor is adjacent to the house, tile is always the decorator's choice.

Outdoor tile is almost always rough-surfaced and usually ¼" to ⅞" thick. Quarry tile makes the best patio floor, and recently Mexican pavers have become popular. These are generally 12″ × 12″ squares, and they are available in various shades of terra cotta coloring.

Most all tiles need a mortar bed, so a concrete floor becomes part of the expense. However, if the area is flat and stable, you might want to lay tile on a bed of sand and earth.

Patio Blocks

Thick patio blocks or pavers are made of concrete that has been vibrated under pressure. They are available in several shapes and several colors. You can install pavers directly on a sand base—very convenient. To install patio pavers:

1. Mark the boundaries with a string and stakes, and remove about 2 inches of soil.
2. Dampen the soil; then add sand and tamp it down. Be sure the sand base is level, and establish a slope away from the house for drainage.
3. Put down a sheet of polyethylene over the sand to prevent weeds or grass from growing between the blocks.
4. Start in a corner to install blocks, and be sure each block is fitted into place absolutely level.

PATIO OVERHANGS

A patio that has a partial roof or overhang becomes a more decorative addition to the home than an open-to-the-sky area. Most patio overheads are constructed with beams, rafters and posts and have a complete or partial covering of wood or canvas. Once the basic frame is built, you can select a covering for it.

Basic construction of a patio overhead begins with laying out the lines on the patio floor. Be sure all corners are square; use a carpenter's level. Mark the locations with stakes on the patio floor, and prepare footings for the posts (dig down at least 18 inches or more, depending upon the frost line in your region). Set the posts in concrete; use a line level and carpenter's level. Mark on the house all the roof lines of the patio overhead. Attach the ledger to the house, and match the posts to the height of the ledger.

CHAPTER THIRTEEN

PLACES FOR PLANTS

Today, "green" is part of the finished home. And places to put plants are an often overlooked aspect of home interiors. But for a finishing touch, add plants. Adding the shelves or nooks or window greenhouses for plants is not expensive, and initial installation is easy. However, few books instruct on where and how to use plants in the home.

Basically, you want plants near windows so they can receive adequate light, and large floor plants in decorative containers are fine, but the smaller plants—window plants—need appropriate shelving. Wall-mounted plant shelves are easy to make and much less expensive than the "kit" shelves available commercially. Window greenhouses and wonderful, old-fashioned window boxes really give the home a finished look—an extra accent that creates an attractive scene.

SHELF GARDENS

The shelf garden is a variation on the window box; our Drawing 13-1 shows a typical type. This design is rather fancy with its curved sidings (the sides can be rectangular also). Lumber used is 2×6 and 2×12 boards, and dowels are placed to support the shelves. With a few potted plants, these are handsome finishing touches to the home.

WINDOW GREENHOUSES

The window greenhouse has become an attractive addition to many homes in recent years. It is an excellent idea because it furnishes proper light for plants. With some minor modifications, almost any window can become an excellent area where plants can flourish, adding beauty and color to a room.

Just what kind of window greenhouse you select depends on four factors:

1. whether you own your home
2. how many plants you want to grow
3. what kind of plants you want to grow
4. how much you want to spend

The window greenhouse can be made inside of existing windows. But for best results, remove the window and frame so the greenhouse extends outside as well as inside. In either case, the face of the greenhouse is angled and made of glass or acrylic in frames with hinged doors for air circulation.

SHELF GARDEN

If your old window trim is monotonous, or if it has been made useless because of a new window installation, this can be a great solution.

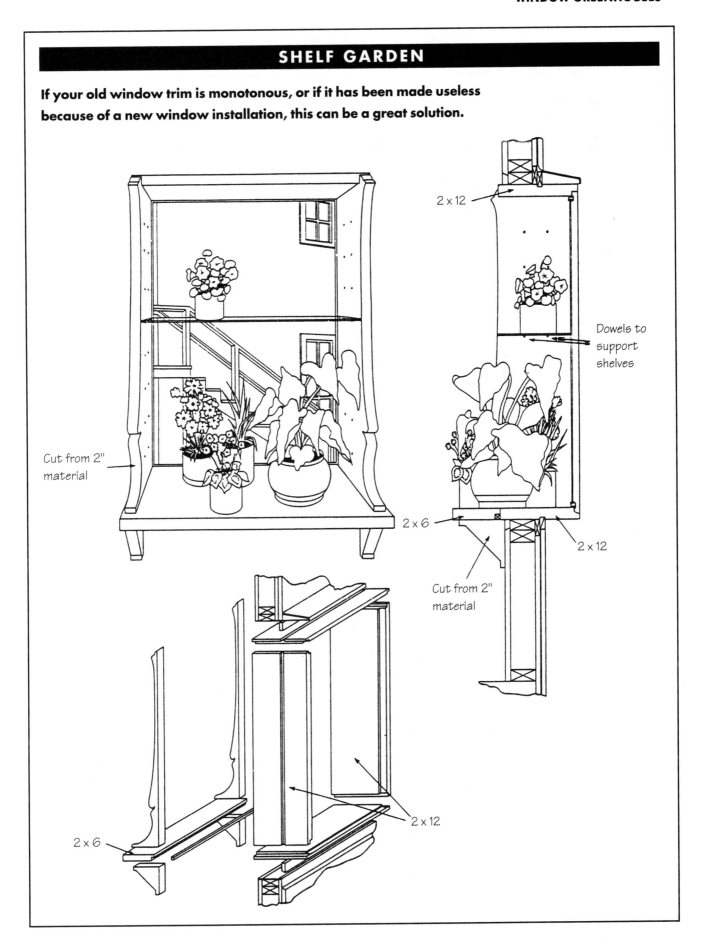

2 x 12

Dowels to support shelves

Cut from 2" material

2 x 6

Cut from 2" material

2 x 12

2 x 12

2 x 6

CHAPTER FOURTEEN

USING WOOD INSIDE

The inside woodwork is more important than one may think at first glance. Actually, interior trim for windows and doors, ceilings and floors says a great deal about the total look. Select and construct these details with care. The interior trim also covers any mistakes you may have made.

The interior woodwork can make or break the remodeling you have done, so again let me caution you to take your time and do it right.

TRIM

Woodwork is an all-encompassing term for *trim*, but basically it involves all trim for floors, windows, doors, ceilings and skylights. Technically, the trim around doors and windows is called *casing*, and that around floors is the *baseboard*. *Wainscoting* is also used as finishing-work to achieve another look. *Molding* is yet another term for trim, and there are an infinite variety of these. Finally, ledges for windows are also a consideration and are, happily, experiencing a renaissance.

Although you can buy many kinds of moldings for casing doors and windows, simple 1×3 or 1×4 pine is often used for a neat look. The standard thickness for window and door trim is $^{11}/_{16}''$ molding, but $2''$ or $3''$ material can also be used depending on your taste. You must also have a window jamb; this is a piece of vertical wood on each side of the window. The standard width of a jamb is $4\frac{1}{2}''$: $3\frac{1}{2}''$ for the stud, plus $\frac{1}{2}''$ each for exterior sheathing and $\frac{1}{2}''$ for interior plasterboard. You would use a wider jamb for a wider wall, say $6''$. The extra space includes a plastered wall with lathing. So jambs can vary; the important thing is that the thickness of the jamb corresponds to the total thickness of the wall.

Windows

A stool or sill is also part of a window and is notched to fit over the sill and butt up against the bottom sash. The width usually extends an inch or so beyond the casing edge. An apron is put under the stool, its length determined by the width of the casing outside to outside.

Of course, different windows call for variation on the general concept—awning and French windows are examples, and casement windows also have special treatment. All basically use the same concepts with slight variations.

Doors

Any interior door worth its weight has distinct trim and is done in the same manner as the windows: Generally doors come with one casing and the thickness of the jamb must correspond to the thickness of the wall.

Moldings

Floor moldings or trim are of various configurations. (See Drawing 14-1.) You can use a simple shoe molding or something more distinctive with rounded edges. The baseboard serves as a bumper against furniture and protects the walls from being marred by cleaning appliances. For ceilings, there are many kinds of decorative trim; the cove moldings are quite handsome, but simple, straight-line moldings can also be used. Your selection depends on the total character of the room and what you are trying to achieve.

Indeed, the variety of moldings for ceilings, walls, floors, doors and windows is so extensive it would be impossible to discuss all of them. In addition, there are general types of trim, such as square and rectangular, half round, quarter round, and so forth. Selecting trim can be interesting and fascinating, so make it fun, not work.

Wainscoting

Wainscoting is somewhat different trim treatment and is used for decorative effect as well. Wainscoting is applying board or paneling to a wall, either at the midpoint or a designated height. It also protects the lower part of the wall from furniture accidentally pushed against it. Wainscoting is usually applied vertically with ¼" paneling placed onto the face of the wall. It can be as high as 4 feet or as low as 2 feet. You can cap the wainscoting with a quarter-round molding at top and bottom, if desired. (See Drawing 14-2.)

INTERIOR MOLDINGS

Numerous patterns and dimensions are produced in a variety of woods. Your lumber dealer should have pamphlets or product sheets describing these and other trim pieces and their availability.

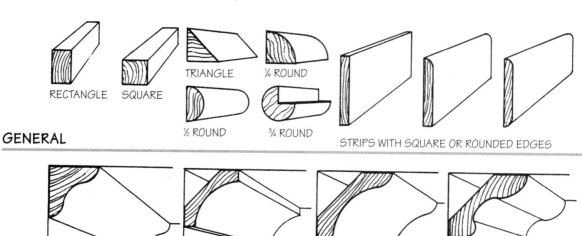

RECTANGLE   SQUARE   TRIANGLE   ¼ ROUND

½ ROUND   ¾ ROUND

STRIPS WITH SQUARE OR ROUNDED EDGES

GENERAL

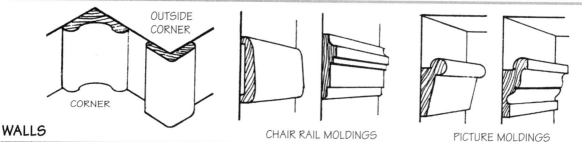

CEILINGS   VARIOUS COVE MOLDINGS

OUTSIDE CORNER

CORNER

WALLS   CHAIR RAIL MOLDINGS   PICTURE MOLDINGS

BASE SHOE

FLOORS   VARIOUS BASEBOARDS

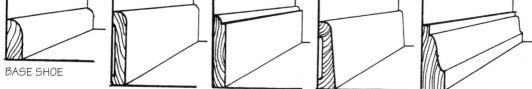

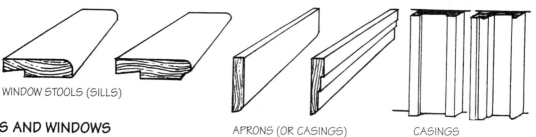

WINDOW STOOLS (SILLS)

DOORS AND WINDOWS   APRONS (OR CASINGS)   CASINGS

WAINSCOTTING

If you want striking wainscotting, don't skimp on ledging or baseboards. By furring the wainscotting out 2-3 inches, you will be able to use large and dramatic ledges and trim pieces.

1 Determine the height (usually 5'). Measure the perimeter, deducting for doorways. Use sheet paneling (4 x 10 panels can be cut in half), or use tongue-and-groove boards.

2 Remove the existing baseboard. Mark a level line measuring down from the ceiling. Then attach the paneling, starting at a corner, by nailing and/or gluing.

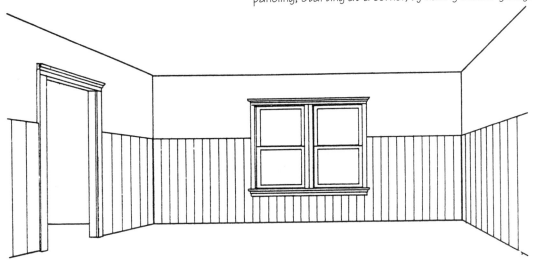

3 Create the top molding and ledge by first nailing a 1 x 2 strip at the top edge of the paneling, then a 1 x 3 on top, with the lower exposed edge rounded, and finally with quarter-round moldings at the joints. Use finishing nails.

Note: The trim should be stained or painted before installing. Countersink the nails and fill with putty. Touch up to match.

4 Create the baseboard with a 1 x 6 nailed at the bottom and trimmed with quarter-round molding on top and at the floor.

5 Use quarter-round molding at the existing door and window trim and at the room corners. Outside corners can be trimmed with a half- and quarter-round combined.

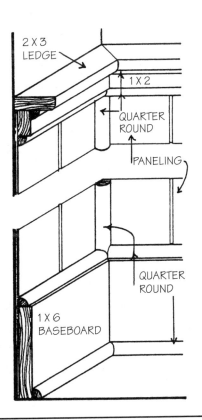

2 X 3 LEDGE

1 X 2

QUARTER ROUND

PANELING

QUARTER ROUND

1 X 6 BASEBOARD

So, for a somewhat different effect, you might want to use the wainscoting concept; it is decorative and adds the craftsperson's touch to a room.

THE TOTAL LOOK

Finishes for wood are varied and numerous, but the selection is not that difficult if you decide what you want beforehand and if you learn a few basics about wood finishes. As you use the various finishes, you will discover more about each product and develop your own tastes. Once you have the rudimentary knowledge, you can experiment and exchange ideas with fellow do-it-yourselfers and hardware- and paint-store personnel.

Filling

Oak, mahogany and walnut are open-grained woods, which means their grains have to be filled for a smooth and even finish. Never use wood putty or plastic—these materials are only for repair work, such as filling holes or covering up chips. Use paste wood filler. This filler has a heavy consistency that is diluted with turpentine or mineral spirits (thinners) and then brushed onto the wood. The filler is absorbed into the grains. Fillers come in assorted wood colors or in natural (clear) finishes and can be brushed onto bare or stained woods.

To start, brush within a small area, working the filler into the grains. The filler has to set—not be dry or wet. You will not be able to wipe away the excess if it is too dry; it will be too wet to work with if it is not dry enough. To test the filler, wipe your finger across the surface of the area, and if a ball forms, the filler is the proper consistency for the next step, wiping.

Wipe away excess filler with a soft cloth, to evenly pack the filler into the grains. Once you have done the first wiping, wipe again with another cloth. Let the wood dry for 24 hours. If after 24 hours you find any excess filler, remove it with a light sanding.

Sealers and Stains

Sealers seal or set the fillers and any stains that you have applied to your project. Sealers that are applied after the fillers prevent moisture absorption. (On wood left natural, the sealer is the first coat applied.)

Stains, which are easy and fast to apply, both color woods and bring their grains to the surface. The color of a stain is denoted by the wood's color: mahogany, fruitwood, cherry or honey maple, for example. But your idea of, say, cherry color may be different from the manufacturer's idea, so carefully study the color charts, and then apply a sample swatch and let it dry to see the final color. If you do much staining, experiment within one brand so you will get to know that manufacturer's colors.

Many people mistakenly think that stains will protect wood, so they do not use waxes, oils or varnishes. Again, let me say that stains are only for color and emphasis of the natural grain. Stains are water-, oil-, spirit-, sealer- or pigment-based. Water stains are transparent dyes dissolved in water. They come in many brilliant, warm colors, are very penetrating, and are easy to apply. Water stains have to dry for 24 hours or more.

Oil stains, which are dyes dissolved in oil, fade a bit after a while, but they are easy to apply and come in many lovely colors. Sealer stains are a combination of sealer with a dye of diluted lacquer, shellac or varnish in a thinner. Sealer stains provide less surface penetration than some other stains.

Spirit stains are dyes dissolved in alcohol, so they dry quicker than most stains. But because of this quick-drying facet, they are hard to apply. The color tones are cool because they dry so fast. Pigmented wiping stains are really surface paints. They are suspended, ground-up paint pigments and so must be mixed well. A wiping stain is very effective for accentuating the grain pattern of wood.

Before you can stain wood, it has to be thoroughly clean and smooth, or any sandpaper grit or roughness will appear on the wood's surface once it is stained. Use bristle brushes or a clean cloth, and start stain work in a hidden spot so you can adjust the color if necessary before you tackle the visible areas. You should work horizontally, on one surface at a time, and avoid edge drip and splatter. If you have to work vertically, do so from the bottom up.

Wood Finishes

As we mentioned earlier, if you are leaving your project natural, all you have to apply is a wood finish. But if you use sealers (and you should) and stains, the finishes are put on last. All finishes will protect wood and make any project handsome. Some finishes adhere only to a wood's surface, others penetrate the wood a bit, and still others get right down to the core of the wood. Here is an overview of the various finishes.

OIL

Bottled, boiled linseed oil imparts a very protective yet natural look. Clean the wood and then pour some oil on the wood's surface. Now rub in the oil with a cloth and steel wool. Repeat the application several times the first day.

For about one month thereafter, oil once a week. Then change to a monthly schedule.

There is also an oil made from boiled linseed oil, turpentine and spar varnish. As with linseed, apply the mixture with a cloth for several weeks until you get the finish you want. Then apply wax (furniture wax, for example) as you would to floors. The result is a hard, durable and handsome finish.

1. Take clear or colored furniture wax and rub it into wood with #0000 steel wool.
2. Wipe off wax and polish with a clean rag.

RESIN

Resin finishes sold under various names sink and penetrate into the wood and provide a tough, resilient surface, one that will withstand abrasions and stains. The finish also beautifies the wood surface by bringing up and slightly darkening the grain.

Apply the resin with a cloth; keep the resin wet for 15 minutes or for the amount of time stated in the directions. Apply a second coat, and when it is dry, wipe away all the resin. These two applications will keep wood almost free of blemishes. But if you do get scratches on wood, just add more resin.

SHELLAC, VARATHANE AND VARNISH

Shellac takes to wood easily, dries quickly, has a nice clarity and resists hard use. Brush on shellac just once; no repeated applications are necessary. White shellac gives a clear, glossy finish, whereas orange shellac colors the wood a bit.

Varathane is clear and easy to apply, and it is probably the most durable and water resistant of all the clear surface finishes. This plastic finish produces a full-bodied toughness and leaves the wood glossy. The synthetic varnishes (spar varnish does not harden well) produce better finishes than oil-based ones. Because varnish dries slowly, dust can settle on it and thus leave a surface not absolutely smooth. If there is much dust in the air, do not use varnish. Brush on varnish in even strokes in one, two or three coats, depending upon your patience. You can sand the wood between each application, but this takes considerable time.

ENAMEL

Enamel, which is available in all sorts of colors from pales to brilliants, gives wood a tough, hard finish. Before applying any enamel, seal the wood with a white enamel-primer undercoat, or make an undercoat of any color by thinning it with four parts enamel to one part solvent. Enamels come in gloss, semigloss and flat finishes, and in water or oil bases. Glossy enamels look best; the flat enamel looks like paint. The water-based enamels (latex) flow on smoothly, dry quickly, and can be removed from your brush and hands with soap and water. However, the oil-based enamels give a better looking color and are more durable.

Always use two coats of enamel, and lay on enamel in one direction rather than brushing it on as you would paint.

Brushes

For all brushed-on finishes, use good bristle brushes, and always clean them thoroughly after you use them. A good bristle brush is expensive but can last for years. Small 3-inch or 4-inch brushes are large enough to cover surfaces but small enough to get into out-of-the-way places.

CHAPTER FIFTEEN

FENCES

Fences provide a finishing touch, a frame for your home. They can be both beautiful and functional for security and privacy. There are many different kinds of fences, but the basic one is made of wood and of simple design you can do yourself.

Picket, basket weave, paneled and board are some types of fences. Once you have decided what kind of fence you need, whether for security or privacy, determine the layout and make a rough pencil sketch on paper to guide layout later. Do check local building codes, because they dictate fence height and placement in relation to setbacks from streets and your neighbor's house. It is also a good idea to consult with your neighbor before you start to build. They may share some of the costs with you.

BUILDING THE FENCE

The actual building of a fence varies somewhat with the design, but basic construction remains almost the same—posts, stringers and boards. One method is to dig holes for posts, set posts in place, attach stringers, and then nail vertical members into place. For a simple fence, this is a good procedure, and one person can do it.

Another method is to assemble the fence in sections—fitting in rails and stringers whenever two posts are in place. In other words, the sections are built on the ground and then lifted and fitted into place.

Mapping/Digging Postholes

Attaching the stringers or rails and the vertical members (boards, pickets, etc.) to the post is the easiest part of fence building. First, however, you must map the course of the fence. Do it this way:

1. Get stakes (wooden pieces sold at lumberyards) and string.
2. Walk the property and lay out the corner stakes.
3. Run string or twine between the stakes, and tie it securely to each stake.
4. Drive in stakes for postholes. Postholes should be located every 6 to 8 feet, depending on fence design.

Once all stakes are in the ground and the fence is mapped out, dig the holes. For this you will need a digging tool called a posthole-digger. You can rent these at rental stores. Digging postholes is hard work, but if you have average strength, you can do it after some practice. If the surface is very rocky, you may have to rent a jack hammer (but this is rare).

Make postholes at least 24 to 30 inches deep. A good rule of thumb is to set posts into the ground at least one-third their length. The width of the hole should be twice the diameter of the post. Make the bottom of the posthole wider than the top so there is a good, solid base for the post. Put 2 to 4 inches of gravel at the bottom of the hole to drain away any water that accumulates in the posthole. This prolongs the life of the wood by helping to prevent rot.

TO SET THE POSTS IN PLACE

1. Shovel some gravel in the hole.
2. Put the post on top of it.
3. Add several shovels of concrete, jiggle the post slightly, and then check the two sides with a carpenter's level.
4. Add concrete so it is flush with the ground; again check two sides with the level.
5. Use a lean concrete mix: one part cement, three parts sand and six parts gravel.
6. Once it is aligned, hold the post by hand for a few minutes.
7. Do not nail on stringers for at least 36 hours (or until concrete is set).

Joints

Be sure stringers or rails are firmly attached to posts, or you will have problems later. The lap joint is the simplest to use to attach the rails to posts; the butt joint is also useful. Hold rails against the posts and toenail them in place. Some perfectionists may prefer the mortised joint where a rectangular hole is cut partly through the post, then the rail is eased into the cut.

Attaching Boards, Other Members

Once the posts and rails are up, the vertical members can be nailed into place. This is easy to do, but it takes time because the spacing must be perfectly uniform. Cut a piece of wood the exact size of the space you want to maintain, and use this as a guide when nailing pickets or boards in place. Do not skimp on nails; use enough to hold the vertical members in place solidly. Allow at least a 2-inch clearance between the bottoms of the vertical members and the top of the soil.

Redwood and cedar are the preferred woods for outdoor construction, and they last many years. Other woods can also be used but will require wood preservatives as protective coatings; you can find these at hardware dealers. There are two kinds: water borne and oil borne.

PREFABRICATED FENCES

The term *prefabricated* means that the design of the fence is already determined; you buy the fence ready to assemble with all components. There are several designs, but remember that when buying "kit" fences, you still generally have to buy the posts also. And any prefabricated fence still takes postholes, layout and so on.

GATES

Gates, like fences, need planning and designing because they, too, are a component of the total landscape plan. Indeed, many times gates can impart a definite mood, formal or informal, to a property.

The choice of a gate will depend on the design of the fence. However, the gate may be of a different material and a different design. Many times it is wise to make the gate design slightly different for visual contrast. The position of the gate is important, too; generally it is placed in close proximity to the house entrance, but this is not mandatory. And don't forget that utility gates somewhere else on the property are wise choices so that deliveries can be made to the house.

Gate Facts

No matter where the entrance is, a definite frame or border—pilasters on each side, or horizontal members, perhaps larger or higher than the fence—is aesthetically pleasing and sets the gate apart while still including it in the fence. The most important factor is that it tells the guest immediately where the gate is. Just how much security you want and how high the fence is will determine the size of the gate. Generally, we think of a gate singly, but gates may also be in pairs — with great effectiveness. Pairs of gates immediately signify the entrance to the house; they are quite handsome where there are long expanses of fence.

The gate or gates will, of course, get more wear and tear than the fence, so it must be built solidly and attached to the fence with heavy-duty bolts and hardware. Hanging the gate so it is straight and plumb will determine whether it opens and closes properly. The average do-it-yourselfer, even with the best intentions, sometimes forgets that in wet weather gates will swell. I know this only too well, because it is the mistake I made in building my own first lattice gates. If possible, have a good carpenter help you with the construction; there is more to it than meets the eye.

Building the Gate

As mentioned, the gate may be of many different patterns and have detailing, but all gates have the same principles of construction. Here are some general rules to follow when building your gate.

First, get the size; measure the space between the gateposts or pilasters at both the top and the bottom. It is imperative that this be square or you will be heading into trouble. If the posts are not square, correct them. Plan the frame width 1 inch less than the opening. For a 48-inch opening, the width of the frame should be 47 inches to allow for swing and hinge space. Now, working on a flat surface, nail and screw together the frame of the gate. Be sure to keep the frame at right angles with a square. Brace the gate with 2 × 4s or suitable lumber. Saw it to fit, and nail the brace at both ends through the horizontal and vertical members (rails). The last step is to nail in place the vertical members, starting at the hinge side of the frame.

Now that the gate is completed, you will have to put hinges in place. Once again, let me mention that you should use heavy-duty hinges — nothing flimsy here. Drill holes in posts and gate frame for the hinges, and screw, or better yet, bolt them in place securely. Fit the gate to the opening by having someone hold it in place for you while you determine whether it swings freely without sagging. Finish by putting latches on.

Hinges and Latches

Hinges and latches determine whether the gate stays in place a year or a day. Use overly strong hinges. Be sure the screws are long enough to really anchor the hinges securely. Use four hinges on all gates over 5 feet in height. Buy weather-resistant hinges: zinc, cadmium, or the popular galvanized kinds so rusting does not stain the gate. There are various kinds of hinges: the butt, the heavy T (which is quite good), the strap hinges, and of course, specially designed hardware if you want to be unique.

As there are many kinds of hinges, there are also many kinds of latches, so think before choosing. Years ago, I though a latch was a latch and that was that. But now, after a few of my gates have been wrecked by storms (or would continually blow open), I realize the value of a good latch. Ring latches are quite good and keep gates secure, but I have found that the thumb latch can come loose in time, causing gates to sag. There are also hasp, bolt, and bolt-and-strap latches.

Many times, the gate is the finishing touch to the total fence and landscaping plan, and while it may seem minor, it does deserve your consideration. We all want the total effect of the setting to be handsome, and that includes an inviting and durable gate.

Glossary

ANCHOR BOLT: A metal spike projecting above concrete, aka "J-Bolt."

BASEBOARD: A board or milled piece nailed onto wall at floor line. Also called *base* and *mop board*.

BASE MOLDING: A band that goes on top of a baseboard as decoration.

BATTEN: A narrow wood strip to cover joints in vertical boards.

BEAM: A heavy horizontal timber or sill supporting floor joists.

LOAD-BEARING WALL: Any wall or partition that supports any load in addition to its own weight.

BENDERBOARD: Thin, flexible, redwood veneer.

BEVEL: An angle cut on a piece of wood or glass.

BLIND NAILING: Nailing through wood so that the nail head will not show, such as through the tongue of a tongue-and-grooved board.

BOARD FOOT: A measurement of lumber: a piece of wood nominally 1″ thick, 12″ long and 12″ wide. A 1 × 12 one-foot long contains one board foot. A 2 × 12 one-foot long contains two board feet.

BRIDGING: Wood or metal members set between floor and ceiling joists midway in their span. *Cross bridging* is a term for members installed in the form of an *X*; *solid bridging* is the term for nominal 2″ members the same depth of the joists themselves and nailed at right angles to the joists.

BUTT JOINT: The point where two wood members butt together, end to end or at right angles. The edges of each member are square.

CANT STRIP: An angled strip installed on 2 × 6 curbs.

CAP: Anything that tops another member. For instance, the top portion of capital of a column or the top pieces of molding.

CASING: Trim for a door or window, nailed to the jamb or wall for a finish.

CAULKING: Pliable material, dispensed from a caulking gun containing a cartridge, to seal seams, joints and cracks, for weatherproofing and waterproofing.

COLLAR BEAM: Nominal 1″ or 2″ boards connecting opposite roof rafters, usually spaced every third or fourth rafter and used to strengthen the rafter system. When collar beams are used for the ceiling under a roof, they are called *ceiling joists*.

CONCRETE SLAB: Poured concrete used as floor.

CORNER BEAD: A metal strip fitting on an outside corner, then plastered. In drywall construction, nailed over plasterboard and finished with joint compound. A bead also can be made of wood to protect and decorate the outside corner.

CORNICE: A boxed structure at the eave line of a roof, consisting of a *facia* (the face of the eave) and a *soffit* (a horizontal member of the eave).

COUNTERFLASHING: Flashing set into brick, usually chimneys, covering shingles and brickwork.

COUNTERSINK: To set the head of a screw or nail at or below the surface.

CRIPPLE STUDS: Vertical 2 × 4s above and below window openings.

CURED: Concrete that has been dried for several days.

DADO: A groove cut across a board.

DORMER: A roofed structure covering an opening in a sloping roof, with a vertical wall with one or more windows. Shed dormers have a sloping roof, with one dimension, and are designed to add more space under a roof. *A or eye* dormers are designed primarily for light and ventilation.

DOUBLE HEADER: A door or window lintel made from two pieces of lumber, placed upright and nailed together.

DOUBLE-HUNG WINDOW: Two sashes installed in vertical grooves that bypass each other when raised or lowered.

DOUBLE STUDS: Double vertical supports.

DRIP CAP: A wood molding set on top of window and door casings to divert rainwater.

DRYWALL: Plasterboard in sheets for interior walls.

FLASHING: Metal placed where the roof meets a wall or masonry and in roof valleys, to weatherproof the joint.

FOOTING: A concrete platform, wider than the foundation, on which the foundation sits. Installed below the frost line to prevent heaving due to freezing and thawing. Can also support a concrete pier or other types of pillars.

FOUNDATION: A wall, usually of concrete or concrete blocks, that sits on the footing and supports the wooden members of the first floor.

FORMS: Wooden members made of plywood and 2 × 4s, or metal, used as retainers for concrete before it sets. Removed after concrete sets. Can be reused.

FRAMING, PLATFORM: A system of wood framing in which each floor is built separately as a platform for the walls. The most common construction of wood-framed houses today.

FROST LINE: The depth to which ground freezes in winter. Ranges from nothing in the deep South to 4 or 5 feet and more in extreme northern areas of the continent. Footings must be placed below the frost line to prevent heaving or movement caused by freezing and thawing.

FULL-HEIGHT STUDS: Vertical 2 × 4s running from floor to ceiling.

FURRING: Strips of wood, usually 1 × 2 or 1 × 3, or metal, used to even out a rough wall and as a base for securing a finished wall, such as plasterboard, plywood paneling or boards.

GABLE: Roof line at the end of a double-sloped roof, forming a triangle from the peak of the roof to the bottom of each end of the rafters.

GIRDER: A heavy beam of wood or steel to support floor joists. Generally set into the sill and supported at intermediate points by columns.

GLAZING COMPOUND: A modern putty

used to waterproof panes of glass in a wood frame.

GRADE: The surface of the ground.

GROOVE: A notch running the length of a board, on the edge.

GROUT: Mortar, with or without sand, used to fill joints between floor or wall tile.

GUSSET: A board connecting rafters butting end to end.

GYPSUM BOARD: A type of plasterboard used to finish interior walls.

HARDBOARD: Manufactured material, made from wood and having wood characteristics, in 4' × 8' sheets and thicknesses of 1/8" and 1/4". Used under resilient tile.

HEADER: A beam placed at right angles to floor joists to form openings for chimneys, stairways, fireplaces, etc. A beam placed as a lintel over door and window openings.

HEADER JOIST: A floor joist connecting the ends of regular floor joists and forming part of the perimeter of the floor framing. Opposite of *stringer joist.*

HIP ROOF: A roof that slopes up from all four sides of a house, meeting at a point in the center of a short ridge. There are no gables in a hip roof.

I-BEAM: A steel beam, named for its profile shape, used to support joists in long spans, and as an extra-long header over windows or doors.

INSULATION: Thermal insulation is placed in wall cavities, in attic floor spaces, and sometimes in cellar ceilings and between roof rafters to reduce escape of heat. It can be fiberglass, rigid or flexible; mineral wood, urethane or sty-

rene; or any other kind of material that reduces heat loss. Sound insulation is of a similar material, mainly fiberglass, and is designed to reduce transmission of sound through walls, ceilings and floors. Reflective insulation is usually aluminum foil in sheet form, designed to reflect heat back into a room and to reflect outside heat in hot weather. It is ineffective unless an air space is provided between it and the interior wall. If it is used at all, it should be used with thermal insulation.

JAMB: The side and top parts of a frame of a window or door.

JOINT: Any space between two components.

JOINT COMPOUND: A type of plaster used to cover nailheads and joints in plasterboard wall construction. The joints are also covered with paper tape.

JOIST: A floor or ceiling beam a nominal thickness of 2", and a depth of 8", 10" or 12", used in parallel to support a floor or ceiling. Floor joists are set on the sill and on girders; if there is a second floor, they are set on top plates of walls. Ceiling joists are set on top plates, and there is no floor secured to them.

JOIST HANGER: A metal fastener used to secure the end of a joist directly against the side of a girder or other joist. Also called timber support.

LAG SCREW: A special screw for plaster installation.

LAP JOINT: A joint in which one member of a doubled beam or plate overlaps the other member. Most common in wall top plates, made up of 2 × 4s, with a lap joint at each corner.

LEDGER: A strip of lumber nailed to a girder or joist onto which other joists are set. Also, a heavy strip nailed to a wall as a joist support.

LINTEL: A horizontal member supporting the opening above a door or window.

METAL LATHING: A grid-pattern metal sheet.

MITER JOINT: A joint made by beveling the ends of the pieces to be joined, usually at a 45° angle, to form a 90° corner.

MORTAR: Material used to hold masonry together, made with Portland cement, sand and lime.

MORTISE: A slot or hole cut into wood to receive the tenon of another piece. The mortise is the female portion of a mortise-and-tenon joint.

MUDSILL: Bottom plate of wall.

MULLION: A vertical divider between two window and (or) door openings.

MUNTIN: Parts of a window sash frame dividing panes of glass.

NAILING BLOCK: A strip of wood attached to a surface to provide a means of attaching another member by nailing.

PARQUET: A patterned floor of an inlay of different geometrically shaped woods.

PENNY: A measurement of nails, originally English, indicated price per 100. Abbreviated *d*.

PIER: A column of masonry.

PLANED: Surfaced and smooth.

PLASTERBOARD: Plaster-type sheeting used as a wall, taped and plastered.

PLATE, SOLE OR FLOOR: The bottom horizontal member of a stud wall, sitting on the subfloor. *Top plate*: the top horizontal member, doubled, of a stud wall, supporting second-floor joists or roof rafters.

POLYETHYLENE VAPOR BARRIER: Plastic sheets used to prevent moisture absorption.

PURLINS: Horizontal members of a roof supporting rafting.

RABBET: A groove at the end of a board, going across the grain.

RAFTER: A beam, nominally 2″ thick, supporting the roof. A *hip* rafter forms a hip of a roof (see *Hip*); a *jack* rafter is a short rafter connecting a hip rafter with the wall top plate, or a valley rafter with the ridge board; a *valley* rafter forms the valley of a roof and usually is doubled.

SHAKE: A thick (split, not sawn) wood shingle, used for rustic siding and normal wood roofing.

SHEATHING: The exterior covering of a wall. Used as a base for siding. Sometimes the sheathing and siding are combined, such as plywood grooved to look like board-on-board or reverse board and batten.

SHEET-METAL WORK: Nearly everything made of sheet metal, such as gutters, downspouts and warm-air ducts.

SHIMS: Tapered pieces of wood, generally shingles, used to close gaps between horizontal and vertical wood spaces, usually along floors and between rough openings for windows and doors and the finish jamb.

SHINGLES: Siding shingles are wood members sawn to a taper, made generally from red or white cedar and tapered from ¼″ at the butt (bottom) to ¹⁄₃₂″ at the top. Roof-ing shingles are made of asphalt, metal, slate, etc. Both types are manufactured to standard sizes.

SHIPLAP: A groove along the side of a board to allow each board to overlap the other but with their surfaces remaining on the same plane.

SIDING: Exterior covering of a wall to keep the weather out and to look good. Various kinds include clapboard, shingle, and board and batten.

SILICONE SEALANT: Special compound sealant for joints.

SILL: Sometimes called *sill plate*: timber sitting directly on masonry foundation; support for floor joists. In windows, the slanting bottom piece of a window frame, designed to shed water.

SLEEPER: A board, nominally 2″ thick, secured to a concrete floor to act as a base for a wood floor.

SOFFIT: The underside of a cornice or boxed eave.

SOLEPLATE: The bottom horizontal board, usually 2 × 6, at floor line.

SPACKLE: Pastelike plaster material for repairing cracks, etc.

STRINGER: Support for cross members of opening in a floor. Parallel to joists. Support for stair treads. A *stringer joist* is the border joist of a floor frame, parallel to intermediate joists. Opposite of *header joist*.

STRUTS: 2 × 2 pieces of wood that support glazing.

STUCCO: Plasterlike siding made with Portland cement as its base. Applied over metal lath.

STUD: A vertical member in a frame wall, usually made of 2 × 4 boards.

SUBFLOOR: Rough boards or plywood

secured to floor joists, onto which a finish floor is secured.

THRESHOLD: A wood or metal member usually tapered on both sides and used between door bottom and doorsill. Also used between jambs of interior doors; not generally used in new housing. Sometimes the threshold is an integral part of the sill.

TIE BEAM: A beam that acts as a tie in a roof.

TIE RODS: Rods used as connecting members.

TIE STRAPS: Metal strips used to join two boards.

TOENAILING: Nailing at an angle, connecting one member with another piece perpendicular to it. Opposite of *face nailing*.

TOGGLE BOLTS: Metal bolts for plaster walls.

TONGUE-AND-GROOVED: A board with tongue on one edge and groove in the other.

TOP PLATE: Horizontal board doubled, usually 2 × 6, above door and window opening supporting second-floor joists or roof rafters.

TREAD: Horizontal board in a stairway that is the part of the step that is stepped on.

TRIM: Finish material on interior and exterior of a house but not including interior walls and exterior siding. Also called *woodwork*.

TRUSS: A set of rafters connecting opposite wall points.

VAPOR BARRIER: Material — aluminum foil, kraft paper or polyethyl-ene — designed to prevent passage of water vapor through or into exterior walls. Always placed toward the heated part of the house. Insulation sometimes is made with a vapor barrier. If not, the barrier is secured after insulation is installed.

WEATHER STRIPPING: Any material placed at window and door seams to prevent passage of air, usually made of wood or aluminum with a vinyl seal.

WING WALL: A wall built at a right angle.

Index